THE

TURK AND THE GREEK;

OR,

CREEDS, RACES, SOCIETY, AND SCENERY IN TURKEY, GREECE, AND THE ISLES OF GREECE.

BY

S. G. W. BENJAMIN.

NEW YORK:
PUBLISHED BY HURD AND HOUGHTON,
459 BROOME STREET.
1867.

RIVERSIDE, CAMBRIDGE:
STEREOTYPED AND PRINTED BY
H. O. HOUGHTON AND COMPANY.

To

THE MEMORY OF

MY FATHER,

WHO CONSECRATED HIS LIFE TO

THE MISSIONARY WORK IN GREECE AND TURKEY, AND NOW

LIES BURIED IN CONSTANTINOPLE, THIS VOLUME IS

REVERENTLY AND AFFECTIONATELY

INSCRIBED.

CONTENTS.

PREFACE.

In the following pages it has not been the intention of the writer to present a continuous narrative of residence or travels, or any elaborate tables of statistics. It has been his aim rather to select such facts and incidents from his experience and observation as seemed to him best adapted to convey to the reader the most vivid impression of the races and countries of the Levant, their character and condition. Allusion to antiquities he has avoided, except in a few instances where mention has been made of such as possess the interest of novelty. So often and so well have the ruins of Turkey and Greece been described, that it would appear presumption to attempt the task anew; nor would the author venture to invite attention to another work on the East, if the public sympathy were not already somewhat aroused about the Cretan Insurrection and the critical condition of the Ottoman Empire.

He has taken the liberty of altering the rendering of foreign names in some cases, seeking to approach as nearly as possible to the native pronunciation, although complete success is naturally out of the question. The arsis in Turkish words has a tendency to fall toward the final syllable, for which reason the syllable so emphasized is in these pages marked by an accent when the mere spelling is insufficient to indicate it. *I* in Oriental names should be pronounced as in French, like long *ē* in bee; *a* is invariably pronounced as in father: the name usually spelt Ali illustrates these three principles; it should be pronounced Ahlēe. The use of the erroneous Saxon long ī sound, in so many Oriental words, when transferred into our language, is probably owing to the circumstance that the French and Italians, preceding us in the Levant, employed their *i* correctly, but in accepting their use of it we forgot the radical difference between the Continental and the Saxon *i*, and adopted what seems the same to the eye but is not an equivalent to the ear.

Chapter VI. is, with some additions, the same as it originally appeared in letters to the "Springfield Republican." The historical sketch of Crete in Chapter X. is a reprint of an article that was recently published in "Harpers' Monthly Magazine;" and the writer has incorporated here and there such extracts from other papers of his in the "North American Review," the "Riverside Magazine," &c., as seemed to him to continue germane to the subject; but the book, for the most part, now appears for the first time in print. Such as it is, the writer commends it to the friendly or adverse criticism of those who find time or inclination to turn over the pages of an unknown work by an untried author.

THE TURK AND THE GREEK.

I.

CONSTANTINOPLE.

MANY years ago the United States frigate *Independence* was sailing up the Marmora toward Constantinople. Dr. Schauffler and the late N. P. Willis were passengers; the former returning to his labors from Smyrna, the other fresh from Naples, and enthusiastic over the beauties of its celebrated Bay. That Constantinople could surpass or even equal Naples seemed to him impossible, and many were the good-natured discussions on the subject during the voyage, until on a fine morning when the rising sun was gilding the domes and clustering spires of the imperial city, the frigate glided majestically by the ancient walls toward her anchorage, while the mellow voices from many a score of minarets floated over the blue waters, calling the faithful to prayer.

Entranced by the magnificence of the scene, Willis stood on the quarter without uttering a word, until Dr. Schauffler said, "Well, what do you think of Constantinople now? Does it equal Naples?" "My dear sir," responded Mr. Willis with fervor, "there is no comparison; Naples is not to be mentioned in the same breath!"

Such were my own feelings when, after an absence of ten years, I again sailed up to Constantinople at sunrise. The grandeur, the magnificence, which had so often thrilled my heart in the days of my youth, were still there. Time had not effaced the beauty that lingers over those ancient battlements and storied seraïs; the purple tints still suffused those winding shores; unfading green still clothed those cypress groves and gardens of delight; the arrowy current still rushed by palaces dreaming over its sparkling waters; swift caïques, manned by picturesque boatmen, still glided hither and thither among the fleets lying at anchor in the stream; and over all hung, as ever, that sky so gloriously blue; while the associations, the scenes, the men, of other times, crowded on the soul and almost overpowered it with rapturous emotions.

It is claimed that the illusion is dispelled

when the traveller lands amidst a hubbub of strange tongues, and finds himself climbing up steep hills and through narrow lanes, where mud and noisome smells and "curs of low degree" abound. That these evils do exist in Constantinople, and that they have a tendency to disenchant those who grumble if they do not everywhere find "modern improvements," is not to be denied. To waste argument on such persons is idle; we do not write for such captious souls. But to those who travel with the laudable resolution to be entertained by what they see, who do not complain if they fail to perceive a resemblance between the Oriental character and Young America, who regard with some veneration customs and ruins around which Time has hung his ivy crown, and see "sermons in stones, and good in every thing," — to such let us say that if they will devote less time to the dissipations of Paris, and remain longer at Constantinople than is usually the case with tourists, they will find themselves well rewarded. They will soon become so familiar with the inconveniences of Eastern life as to disregard them, and will even learn that many customs that are novel and perhaps therefore disagreeable at first, are in reality advantages suggested by the climate.

In proportion as the traveller becomes familiar with Oriental habits he will be entertained and instructed by what he sees.

At first, of course, the stranger in Constantinople, ignorant of its innumerable dialects, of the sinuosities of its narrow streets, of the character of its people, and of its principal objects of historic interest, must necessarily commit himself to the tender mercies of a garrulous and not over-scrupulous cicerone, and go through a stereotyped order of sight-seeing, all of which, however, will be novel to him. It is well to obtain at once a distinct outline of the main features of the capital, of which the details can afterward be filled in at one's leisure. In drawing this mental sketch of the chief objects of attraction in a place of such historic interest, where every spot reminds us of past events, it may be some assistance to keep in mind that the history of Constantinople since the Christian era is divisible into two great epochs, — the rise and fall of the Lower or Byzantine Empire, and the rise and decline of the Ottoman Empire, — between which there are striking points of analogy. Within comparatively a short period the former reached the summit of its glory, distinguished by the fortunate reign of Justinian, who, by the aid of

Belisarius, Narses, and other successful soldiers, maintained and somewhat enlarged the limits of his vast dominions. In like manner, in a few generations the Turkish power culminated in the reign of Sulymân the Magnificent, the noblest of his line, who by the force of his arms enlarged and consolidated the conquests of his predecessors. With a grasp of intellect which comprehended the welfare of later generations, both monarchs devoted their genius to the creation of a code of laws as a basis for the permanent and prosperous existence of their people, which, notwithstanding numerous defects, would have been sufficient to sustain the national vigor for a long period, if their precepts had been properly observed. Both sovereigns give us examples of the highest virtue that has been attained by dynasties infamous for their crimes; each bestowed his life-long affections on one woman, and as if in mockery of such ill-timed fidelity, and as if to show the rottenness of the public morals, these two women, Theodora and Roxelana, were unworthy of the love that they retained until death, but abused, to subserve their own selfish ends. As though to furnish a tide-mark whereby posterity could measure the height which the Greek and the Turk have reached, and from what a pinnacle of glory they have fallen, Justinian and Sulymán erected respectively the church of St. Sophia and the mosque of Sulymánié, under the superintendence of Anthemius and Sinán, the greatest architects of Byzantium and Stambûl; on each edifice were lavished the treasures of the Orient, and each is the masterpiece of the styles which they represent, — the Byzantine and the Turko-Saracenic.

These two monuments of glories that have vanished forever, are the central points of historic attraction in Constantinople. They suggest to the beholder nearly all that is eventful in her past. St. Sophia has existed thirteen hundred years, and has been in the hands of the Moslems only a little over four centuries. The central church in Christendom, unsurpassed in the magnificence of its architecture, as seen from within, — for the buttresses built up to sustain the venerable edifice, weakened by earthquakes and age, somewhat mar its exterior, — it still stands, the magnet toward which are turned the longing eyes of the Eastern Christians, who are steadfastly awaiting the hour when the great bell of Time shall toll the doom of Islám, and when the golden cross shall again and forever replace the crescent on that immortal dome, beneath whose vaults the anthem of praise first pealed thirteen centuries ago. The Greeks have a tradition that a priest who was administering the sacrament when the Turkish host burst into the sacred edifice, was snatched away by an angel and concealed within a crypt in the walls of the building, where he patiently abides the day when the departure of the Mohammedan will summon him forth from his hiding-place, to complete the mass which he was performing. It is a noteworthy fact that not only St. Sophia, but most of the other antiquities of Constantinople, remind us rather of the dominion of the Greek than of the subsequent rule of the Turk. The city walls, at least forty of the mosques, and even large portions of the famous bazaars, are of a date anterior to the Turkish conquest. Many of the local names are simply Tartaric adaptations of Greek appellatives, and everywhere along the Bosphorus events are suggested to memory and imagination that occurred in remote periods up to the very dawn of history.

The mosque of Sulymánié, the finest specimen of the exquisite Saracenic architecture of which so many choice examples are to be seen in many of the mosques, fountains, and mausoleums of Constantinople, has been recently repaired, and is well calculated to give some idea of the most glorious period in the history of Turkey. It rivals, if it does not surpass, St. Sophia. It is doubtful whether there exists in architecture a more perfect combination of symmetry, beauty, and sublimity than the view under the dome of Sulymánié. The building stands on a platform or terrace on the highest of the seven hills of Constantinople, from whence may be obtained one of the most impressive prospects of the city, its port, and its suburbs. How often Sulymán must have stood on this terrace, his bosom swelling with exultation as he gazed upon the magnificent spectacle at his feet, which owed so much of its prosperity and splendor to his genius. The tombs of Sulymân and his well-beloved wife Roxelana are in a little inclosure within the precincts of the mosque court. Here one may read an instructive lesson on the greatness and the littleness of man. One of the noblest of the Seljuks had inscribed for his epitaph: "O ye who have seen the glory of Alp Arslan exalted to the heavens, repair to Meru, and you will behold it buried in the dust."

But the present, as well as the past, affords interest to those who regard Constantinople with a reflecting eye. History, as related in books, is to the many but an abstraction, and to repeople its monuments with vanished generations requires a certain effort of the imagination irksome to most travellers. But the present, real, living, tangible, — there is something that appeals to the sympathies of all; — these hurrying throngs, these shifting phases of social existence, these events constantly enacted before us on the world's stage, — these fascinate our gaze and both divert and instruct us. And after all, the teeming humanity packed in this vast city, that combines in itself the customs and character of the past with the innovations of our day, and suggests the probable changes of the future, what is it but history? He is the best historic painter whose canvas delineates current events for the instruction of posterity; he is the best student of Oriental history who investigates the races of the East as they are; thus can he most intelligibly understand her as represented in her records, and thus also estimate the possibilities of her hereafter.

The Golden Gate and the Golden Horn, San Francisco and Constantinople, are the most remarkable cities of our age, the most characteristic of the two forms which distinguish the progress of our day. Cities destined by position to be the great marts of trade, the centres of civilization, each the queen city of half a world: in the one we see the genius of the West reigning undisturbed; in the other we behold him, young, ardent, and irrepressible, returning to the birthplace of his sires and seeking to assert his heirship to the Orient as well as to the Occident, and striving to infuse the elixir of life into the stagnant veins of the effete races of eld. At Constantinople the East and the West, the Past and the Present, old age and sturdy manhood, have met in the decisive grapple, and it resembles

> "The strife which currents rage
> Where Orinoco in his pride
> Rolls to the main no tribute tide,
> But 'gainst broad ocean urges far
> A rival sea of roaring war,
> While, in ten thousand eddies driven,
> The billows fling their foam to heaven."

The scream of the steam-whistle blends in Constantinople with the voice of the improvisatore, who repeats tales similar to the "Arabian Nights" to enraptured groups in the coffee shops. A famous story-teller of this kind died recently, who received a thousand piasters a night for his improvisations, and was always in request whenever a marriage or a festival was to come off in high life. So they did in the days of Haroún al Rescheed, but lest the listener to these romantic tales should fancy himself in the past, the telegraph-wires cross the streets overhead, transporting messages from San Francisco to Bombay, and remind him that this is the nineteenth century A. D.

The Galata Bridge, that, by a cordon of boats, spans the Golden Horn between the Christian quarter called Galata and the old city or Stambûl, is on the whole the most interesting spot in the world to observe the conflict between the old and the new alluded to above, and to study diverse races and kindreds and tongues. What the quays of Venice were in her prime, when she traded with all nations, such is the Galata Bridge, only in a more marked degree. Here is a Circassian, with his fair face, symmetrical figure, curious costume, and mediæval weapons, — a sort of anachronism fresh from the Caucasus; there hurries along a Yankee captain, with a tawny tuft on his chin, spitting as none but Americans spit, and cursing these Turks for lazy dogs; yonder rides a Nubian eunuch mounted on a superb barb and followed by white outriders; and here goes an English lord, proud of his patrician blood. A barouche drawn by Hungarian horses contains the harém of a pashá in green and orange *feredges* and gauze veils, scarcely concealing beautiful profiles, and near by walks a Frank lady dressed in the latest Parisian fashion, and with the most approved style of *chignon;* a rough Koord jostles the fair daughter of a Fifth Avenue millionaire, and the half-naked fakir, or Mohammedan mendicant friar, whose original complexion is lost under a layer of filth and tan, long black elf-locks hanging over his low forehead, a brutal glare in his wicked eye, a pointed iron in one hand, and a shell in the other, which he holds out for alms while guttural sounds proceed from his chest, brushes his lousy rags against the homely but spotless attire of a deaconness from Kaiserwerth. That gypsy girl, who has the shrewdness to allow her veil to slip from off her comely features and thereby wins many paras from the passers-by, excites a smile as her bold behavior shocks the proprieties of the portly and very reverend brother of the Jesuit mission whose flowing skirts she half arrests in her appeal for money; a hamâl or porter laden with planks stretching far in his front and rear, and shouting "saoôl," rather disturbs the meditations of a grave savan from Berlin, whose spectacles he grazes with the end of his load; a crafty-looking Persian from Ispahan, in conical cap, and crying camel's-hair shawls for sale, offers his wares to a lovely exile from Warsaw; and the balustrades of the Bridge are lined with idlers from every nation under heaven. Beautiful English-built steamers are moored to the Bridge alongside of quaint vessels from the Euxine; and the black-eyed Greek boy calls out the evening paper while the muezzin's voice proclaims that "There is no God but God, and Mahomet is his prophet."

Aye, the world does move. There are boot-blacks now in the streets of the capital of the Grand Turk, which is one of the most reasonable innovations ever introduced there from the West, as this city is no less famous for its mud than for its fires or its external splendor. But this is not all; within a few years every street and house in Constantinople and its suburbs has been named and numbered, and the European quarters, called Pera and Galata, are now lighted with gas. It follows from this that the main streets are now used for promenades to a late hour, and localities which in former times it was imprudent to traverse after dark without a revolver, are now comparatively safe. Signs of change that are still more wonderful are observable, here and there, making a ripple on the stagnant waters of national prejudice, superstition, and sloth. The wives of some of the Pashâs have adopted the European dress, wearing the native costume only when they emerge into the street; and whereas it has formerly been considered non-essential for a woman even to read, there are now a number of schools in Constantinople established for Turkish girls, in some of which French and other foreign languages are taught, after a fashion. Although these innovations are confined chiefly to the capital, and doubtless seem ridiculously insignificant to the uninitiated, thirty years ago the mention of such reforms would have appeared as absurd as was the steam-engine to our ancestors, and none who valued their interests would have dared to propose them. There are many still living who can recall the time when the Janissaries were in power and would have demanded the head of any one so bold as to suggest these modern intrusions on the spirit of Eastern and Mohammedan customs.

Soon after my arrival in Constantinople, and toward the close of the terrible cholera season, occurred a series of conflagrations such as are frequent in that city. The most destructive of these fires consumed over three thousand houses. The government made this the occasion for the initiation of a great reform in the Turkish laws concerning property. All the real estate in the burnt district which by the Turkish law of mortmain had become Vakoof, or mosque property, was secularized. It is estimated that by the action of these laws a third of the realty of the empire has gradually become vested in the hands of the Mussulman priests and monks, as has been the case in Italy. By this means a large number of lazy, sensual, fanatical vagabonds are maintained, who are naturally opposed to every sign of progress, and are so numerous as to constitute a dangerous element in society, and act as a check on any impulses toward reform which may move either individuals or the public. In addition to taking away the power of these monks, the abolition of the efkáf or law of mortmain would materially increase the revenues of the government besides allowing corporate bodies to hold landed property, which would be a long step in advance. For years the Porte has been laboring to bring the clerical or old school party under its control, but it is a measure requiring shrewdness and management. The edict to which we have alluded may be considered an entering wedge toward the accomplishment of this great object.

Another advantage resulting from the fires that within a few years have devastated Constantinople is the circumstance that the government has made them the opportunity to rebuild many portions of the city in a style less picturesque, but more durable, than the usual mode of Constantinople architecture. These improvements have been extended into some of the unburnt districts, and it will not surprise those who are conversant with the Orientals to learn that when buildings are trimmed off or torn down for the purpose of widening the streets, no compensation is allowed the owners.

But while there is thus evidenced a certain effort toward decreasing the destructiveness of fires in Constantinople, little improvement is introduced in the mode of extinguishing them. No city could be much worse off in this respect. There are two fire-towers on the highest points on each side of the Golden Horn. One of these is an old Genoese fortification in Galata; the other is a Turkish structure, rather effective than otherwise, as it soars several hundred feet above the water. In the galleries of these towers watchmen walk day and night, spy-glass in hand. On the discovery of a fire a red ball is hoisted in the day-time, and a red lantern at night, from a flag-staff above, and guns are also fired from a battery on the Bosphorus. The alarm is then given to all the police stations, and runners are sent throughout the city and its suburbs who call attention by beating the pavement with iron-shod staves, and follow this by crying "YANGUN VÁR," "There is fire!" giving out also the location of the conflagration. Nothing can be more impressive than this alarum ringing far and wide throughout the silent streets at dead of night and bringing terror to many a heart. I remember hearing this cry five times on a wild winter's night in my boyhood, and on rushing up to the top of the house, seeing the sky ablaze like an oven and the snow-covered roofs red as blood, while the crash of falling houses, and the shouts and shrieks of multitudes, as in a battle, mingled with the warring sounds of the elements. Eighteen hundred houses were destroyed that night. As soon as the alarm is given the fire-engines are borne to the scene of action; but they are of little use, for they are only three or four feet square, small enough to be carried on the shoulders of the firemen, who rush through the narrow streets stripped to the waist and yelling like demons. These firemen receive little or no regular pay, but, excepting a backsheesh at the New Year, are dependent on the owners of burning houses for the remuneration of their services. The bargain goes on amidst a vast deal of Oriental chaffering, and ten to one, before an agreement is reached, the building in question has vanished into smoke and ashes.

II.

MOSAIC.

AS suggested in the previous chapter, there is much remaining to invite the attention of the stranger in Constantinople after he has paid his respects to St. Sophia, Sulymanié, the old armory of St. Irené and the other monuments of antiquity usually shown to travellers. Having now become "master of the situation," let him shake himself free from the conventional jargon of his guide, and wander at will through the mighty city; he will thus discover many an object that escapes the eye of the ordinary tourist. Idling in the coffee-shops, the baths, the bazaars or on the quays, he will have ample opportunity to study the character of the people, and will frequently observe incidents and traits that recall well-known passages in the Bible or the Arabian Nights, and it will seem to him as if he were living in past ages. Familiar as I had become with the details of Oriental life by a long residence in the Levant,

I was still often surprised on revisiting the East, to find how many peculiarities, novel in my experience, were constantly coming to my knowledge. The spirit of the romantic Orient only reveals herself clearly to him who approaches her with reverence, and with leisure rightly to contemplate her charms.

Let the true and earnest searcher after something new stroll through the streets as if by a pleasant exception to the laws of mortality he were to live "two Methuselahs" and were in no wise hurried: the weekly fair in the Pershembé Bazaar, or in the court of the Yenee Jamee, where curiously shaped and gaily colored slippers, vestments of various sorts, mimic mountains of tobacco, censers, kettles, and samovars of brass, perfumeries, and other Oriental wares are temptingly displayed in booths or on mats under the trees, and a throng of buyers are clustered around like bees on a field of thyme, will afford endless amusement to the observant stranger. The booth where a grave old Turkish scribe, seated cross-legged, a pair of goggles on his aquiline nose imparting an owlish air of sapiency to his countenance, and with a scriptural inkhorn and reed pens is writing letters for a group of women who are dictating to him, presents another of the many objects of interest in Constantinople; then there is the Bazaar where they sell old arms, in which the virtuoso may find ample material for his entertainment. There may be seen maces that have battered Christian skulls in the wars of olden time, and blades of Damascus and Korassán, with the beautiful wavy lines distinctly visible on the matchless steel, and with hilts mounted with precious metals and gems. Spears and huge flintlocks from Koordistán, yataghans from Albania, and every variety of Oriental weapons of the past ages, may also be bought there for reasonable prices and examined for nothing. The makers of tobacco pipes and other utensils amuse the observer by the skill with which they produce exquisite results with very primitive tools; the confectionery shops are ever presenting their seductive stores of bacclavâ, a sort of pastry, and rahat-el-lo-koom, falsely-so-called fig paste, a curious misnomer, for there is no fig in the composition of this delicious delicacy, which is very different from the article that passes for it in America: often, too, when wandering in the old city, the traveller will find himself near the mosque of Sultan Bayazíd, whose beautiful Saracenic gates and cloisters will invite him in to watch the feeding of the doves. Many years ago a pious pilgrim brought from Mecca a pair of sacred pigeons, so the legend runs, and deposited them in the precincts of this mosque. Now, as one enters the court, he hears a loud cooing from all sides, and is delighted at seeing the capitals of the pillars, the eaves, and the branches of the trees, populated by hundreds of doves, all of a slate color, protected from harm by the Mohammedan prejudice in favor of animals. Fearless of the artisans working below, or of those traversing the court, thus they pass their quiet and happy lives. If a little grain is thrown upon the pavement, the whirr of a thousand pair of wings is heard as the whole feathered colony swoops down to feed.

When the afternoons are pleasant, and for nine months out of the twelve few of any other sort occur, nothing can be more charming than to walk out to the Armenian cemetery of Pera; a coffee-house on the brow of the height commands a superb view over the palace of Beshiktâsh, Scutari, the Marmora, and Stambûl, and is a favorite resort of the Franks. One may thus have a good opportunity of observing this peculiar although least interesting portion of the many races of Constantinople. Like the Creoles of Mexico, they usually retain the vices of the countries from whence their fathers came, with the low morals of their Greek or Armenian mothers. Versatile, mercurial, ready at picking up languages, and apt in amassing money by fair means or foul, they are never profound, are rarely actuated by ennobling sentiments, are mean-spirited, and can fairly claim nothing in common that savors of national feeling except a narrow bigotry for the Romish Church on the part of the women, and infidelity on the part of the men. It is to be said in their favor that their women are often very pretty and piquant in their manners, especially they of the lower classes whose mothers were Greeks.

First contact with the masses that compose the population of Constantinople must necessarily have a bewildering effect on the mind. The confused fragments of a Chinese puzzle, the disjointed bits of glass of a broken kaleidoscope, a printer's type thrown into "pi," are not less without order or form, apparently, than the motley crowds that whirl ceaselessly through the singular streets of this Vanity Fair, like the ever-moving procession that Vathek saw in the Halls of Eblis. Babel seems reënacted as one beholds representatives from every nation between Pekin and

Chicago pass before him, and hears almost every variation of language spoken since the flood. Nor does a cursory inspection afford much assistance in unravelling this tangled skein of life. The Turkish language is almost universally spoken or understood, as it is the tongue of the dominant race, for the Turks have always disdained to acquire the dialects of their subjects; but, at the same time, the signs in Pera are often printed in several languages, the shop-keepers of the bazaars speak half a dozen in as many minutes to as many customers of different races, and if one attends an evening party he may have the opportunity of hearing a lively conversation conducted alternately in languages enough to throw Mezzofanti into raptures. Ostensibly the government is Turkish, but its Grand Viziers are generally Christian slaves, its bankers are Armenians and Jews, its general-in-chief, Omér Pachâ, is a Croat, and many of its civil, military, and naval officers are Negroes, Arabs, Armenians, Sclaves, Greeks, Frenchmen, Germans, Italians, Englishmen, and even Americans. The Turks of Constantinople are themselves Turks in little more than name and religion; their system of polygamy, and of elevating the female slaves captured in war to the dignity of wives, has so diluted the blood of the few Turks who originally came into Asia Minor with Othmán, that the number of genuine Turks in the Empire is small, and of those born in Constantinople it is doubtful if there is one who cannot claim foreign blood in his veins. For this reason, and on account of the somewhat Europeanized costume now worn by the Constantinopolitan, it is more difficult than formerly always to distinguish Turks at a glance from Armenians or Greeks. In other parts of Turkey grand specimens of the Turkish race are often seen, large of frame, with manly and martial features, men who render it easy to understand the power that once made the crescent a terror to Christendom. But the Turk of Stambûl is pale and effeminate, although handsome in his appearance, denoting his descent from enslaved races, and the corrupting effects of low sensuality. He respects neither the Koran nor the Bible; wine, opium, women, and vices without a name are the pursuits of his life, and, following the example of the Christians of the East, cunning and knavery are the principles on which he transacts his business. How has the mighty fallen! Exceptions of course exist, and the Turks who have embraced

Christianity within a few years at the risk of their lives, exhibit the virtues which rightfully belong to the original stock from whence they came, and show of what the race is capable under favorable circumstances; but we do not speak of these.

It is generally supposed that the traditional jealousy that watches over the life of the Turkish female, places it out of her power to behave indiscreetly. The seclusion of the harém, the latticed windows, the gauze veils drawn over the face when abroad, the vengeance impending on the discovery of conjugal improprieties, are considered as ample safeguards to their virtue. But this is a mistake. They are allowed to frequent the places of public resort with freedom so long as they are veiled, and thus disguised it is difficult to recognize them; and no man can lift the veil of a woman in the street without risking his life. During the Crimean war a drunken French soldier stepped up to a carriage and raised the yashmák of one of the inmates; her attendants cut him down on the spot. It is evident that thus disguised women may go where they please during the day-time without the knowledge of their husbands; and they are to be seen everywhere, groups in gayly colored dress, shopping in the bazaars, eating mahalabee under the trees of the Sweet Waters, or gliding up the Bosphorus in gilt caïques, usually attended by their children, and, if of high rank, accompanied by one or more eunuchs and footmen. Often they may be heard chattering and laughing in the streets in a manner betokening easy adaptation to the singular life they lead. It is evident that theirs is not a life suited to stimulate the growth of either virtuous actions or thoughts. Married to men they have never seen before, often purchased concubines, rarely treated as equals or companions but simply as kept mistresses, bickering among themselves for the favor of their lord, almost as ignorant as children, and possessed of the warm passions of the East, with no mental or moral education to elevate their thoughts, it is but a natural result that they should be low in their tastes and depraved in their lives. Intrigue and assignations are every-day affairs, for part of which the Franks of Pera are responsible. As in many races that retain more or less of their barbaric origin, the Turkish female is generally of an inferior mould to the male, and the early arrival of puberty and marriage cause a correspondingly early decay of their beauty. It is rare to find a Turkish woman who retains her good looks beyond thirty-five, while I have seen many Turks who were strikingly noble in their mien and features in old age. The Turkish woman, however, is not destitute of strength of character, and under favorable circumstances has been seen to develop a conjugal devotion, a maternal solicitude, and a heroism such as often render the daughters of the West very nearly the compeers of the sterner sex in mental capacity, and too often their superiors in the susceptibilities or emotional part of our nature, the highest attribute of the soul.

One trait the Turk inherits in a marked degree from the pastoral life of his ancestors, — a strong love for children; a sentiment so lively and universal in the East, that it is considered an affliction of Providence for married people to be childless. All the more horrible, for this reason, is the custom of the royal line of Turkey, which ordains that the male children of the Sultan's sisters or nieces should be killed at their birth. The throne, by a singular law, is inherited by the collateral heirs, if there should be any living, before the Sultan's own son can succeed him; on this account the brothers and nephews of the reigning Sultan have for many generations been bowstrung to prevent any disturbances against his authority. The sister of Abdûl Medjíd, married to Haleel Pashâ, lost two sons in this way during her father's life. Abdûl Medjíd, a man of rare clemency for an Oriental, was the first to disregard this atrocious custom. He allowed his brother, Abdûl Azíz, to live in great seclusion, and he in turn, moved probably by this precedent and the improved state of public opinion, rather than by his natural disposition, allows his nephew, the son of Abdûl Medjíd, and heir apparent to the throne, to live and enjoy a measure of liberty at the capital; but his life would be the forfeit for the slightest indiscretion.

The corrupt morals of Constantinople are not entirely confined to the Mohammedan population. Vice does not perhaps display itself so alluringly nor so publicly as in certain quarters of Paris or London, but there is a more general absence of propriety, if possible, in business, conversation, and the social relations, which pervades all ranks and races. The heart of society is rotten to the core; integrity, either private or public, is rare; principle is at a discount, vice at a premium; the first and indispensable qualification for a clerk in the bazaars is that he should be a clever liar. There is not very much choice between the virtue of the Turks and the native Christians; the former are more gross in their appetites, more stolid in their comprehensions, while the latter in their knavery are more adroit and cunning; *timeo Danaos et dona ferentes*. There is a thin varnish of suavity, an ease and grace of deportment, a winning plausibility characteristic of all the races of the Orient, in consonance with the softness of the clime, often rendering them agreeable, and well adapted to deceive the more sincere foreigner who is off his guard, but too frequently it is only the enamel that scarce conceals the false face of the syren. Better the blunt honesty of John Bull that, under a harsh exterior, contains the genuine heart of a true man, than the supple courtliness which masks a caitiff heart.

Another feature noticeable in the character of Constantinople society, is the almost total absence of public spirit. This arises from the circumstance that, figuratively speaking, every man's hand is against his neighbor. In the capital, as throughout the empire, we see the people divided into conquerors and conquered, oppressors and oppressed, and a war of races is the natural result. The Turk, while often having Christian slaves for his mistresses, has never legally intermarried with the subject races, and differences of sect have kept them also from coalescing and making common cause against their oppressors; the Gulf Stream does not preserve its current more distinctly from the surrounding ocean, than the many nations of Turkey have guarded their individuality through long ages of misrule. As a consequence the Armenian regards the Greek with jealousy, and the Greek in turn regards the Armenian with distrust, each watching lest the other acquire undue influence at the Porte, and both unite in cursing the Turk; while he hates them as Christian dogs who may eventually oust him from his dominion over them. It is easy to see of what discordant elements the million inhabitants of Constantinople and its suburbs must be composed. The reforms to which we have alluded have as yet done very little to abolish this clannish and unprogressive condition of society. The Moslems still dwell for the most part in Stambûl, Scutari, and Kassím Pashâ; the Jews still huddle together in the filthy lanes of Balát; the Greeks still affect the dark but historic precincts of the Fanár; the Armenians still most do congregate in Yení Kapoo; and the Franks or Latins continue to build their European mansions on the salubrious heights of Pera.

This state of things is any thing but conducive to the encouragement of a healthy tone of the public mind, and also imparts a certain insecurity to municipal affairs. The body politic is too much like the image in Nebuchadnezzar's dream, composed of materials so incoherent that a blow would resolve it into a confused mass of antagonistic elements. Suspicion and distrust enter into all the intercourse and transactions of the Constantinopolitan. The French law proceeds on the assumption that the criminal at the bar is guilty until he has made his innocence good. In like manner in the East, until a man has proved his integrity beyond a doubt, it is safe to presume that if it is for his interest to do so, he will cheat or injure to the extent of his ability; and every one therefore shapes his actions more or less with the principle of self-defense in view. It is for this reason that immediately on leaving the limits of Constantinople, or any other Oriental city, the country seems almost uninhabited, except as a village is found here and there on an eminence. The unsafe condition of society, combined with the rude and scarce means of communication, forbids people to live on solitary farms at a distance from a town, as often happens in the rural districts of Europe and America; and ordinary prudence suggests that those who care to ride or promenade beyond the outskirts of the city should go armed, as many, the writer included, have learned from personal experience. An Englishman last summer took a sail-boat manned by two Ionian Islanders for Prinkipo. As he had addressed them in Turkish, they supposed him ignorant of Greek, and in that language he had the pleasure of hearing the discussion of a plot to assassinate him, and after robbing to throw his body into the sea and conceal themselves for a few days at the Dardanelles, until the excitement from his disappearance had blown over. When they had thoroughly digested the plan, and just as they were about to put it into execution, he drew his revolver, and swore to them in Greek that the first who stirred was a dead man.

But while there are so many evils arising from this antagonism of races, it gives pleasure to those who are fond of studying national traits, of observing different physical types, and of enjoying the artistic effect produced by an ever-shifting variety of costumes. Far more picturesque is a crowd in Constantinople than in New York, where all are clad in the sombre and convenient but ungainly garb suggested by the cold climate and passionless races of Northern Europe and America. All tints and colors blend in the streets of Constantinople, and well do they harmonize with the softness of the climate, the azure skies of noonday, and the glory of sunset. Our western civilization, noble and elevating as it is, has yet a freezing influence on all that is picturesque and artistic; a block of Fifth Avenue mansions or a group of merchant princes may look elegant and intelligent, but the sensitive eye of the artist turns from them to rest with infinite delight upon a row of quaint, antique, many-gabled houses lazily standing along the shores of the Bosphorus, or a knot of indolent Turks dreamily smoking under the spreading foliage of the vale of the Flamoors, while gaily dressed maidens, reclining on the grass, quaff sherbet, and fill the soft air of May with their ringing laughter.

There is a costume that has of late become very frequent in Constantinople, the Circassian. A felt cap surrounded by a shaggy roll of sheepskin, surmounts a face almost femininely fair and delicate in its complexion and outline; a drab coat with flowing sleeves drops below the knee, and is held together by a belt around the slender waist; on each breast is a brass or silver-mounted cartouche box; at the left side hangs a scimetar; at the right side a very curious, antique, richly-mounted flint-lock pistol is suspended by a cord of gold and silken braid; a dagger is carried in the belt, and a pair of leggins and red buskins complete the dress of the warriors who, under the guidance of Schamyl, held the fastnesses of Daghestán so many years against the Czar of all the Russias. In the time of battle they sometimes wear in addition a chain hauberk, such as was in use during the days of chivalry.

It may not be generally known that after the Russians had subjugated the Circassians, many thousands of that unfortunate people emigrated to Turkey, whether voluntarily or by compulsion being a matter of uncertainty. They were received with some hospitality by the Turkish government, and assigned rude shanties, and appointed to till the soil in various parts of the Empire, either on the public lands or in villages from which the inhabitants were ejected or obliged to share their hovels with the new comers, which has naturally given rise to many disturbances. These Circassians, by the way, are a study for the ethnologist. They are composed of many distinct tribes, instead of forming one compact nation, and each tribe speaks a dialect scarcely intelligible to any but the chiefs. Their social system resembles the feudalism of the Middle Ages, each tribe being under the rule of a prince, who receives the homage of a number of feudal lords who hold the people in serfdom. With the exception of the chiefs, who are Mohammedans, the mass of the people are worshippers of heathen deities; one of these is a certain wood-goddess resembling Melita; what little is ascertained of their religion reminds one of the worship of the Druids in Britain and Gaul.

It is well known that for long the far-famed beauty of the Circassian females has caused Circassian slaves to bring a high price in the slave-markets of the East; and although for some years past the trade has been nominally forbidden at Constantinople, it is still practised in a corner, and winked at by the authorities. The influx into Turkey of so many Circassian exiles, ignorant of the language, poverty-stricken, and in search of a home, was an opportunity for the slave-dealers, which they seized with avidity. Girls of rare beauty have been purchased on the shores of the Black Sea for a mere pittance, been educated to a certain degree, and then resold to grandees at enormous profits.

On a wild night when snow and rain were falling, and the streets, famed for their mud, were more miry than ever, and but few ventured out into the storm, a slave-dealer was crossing the Galata Bridge, urging along a young Circassian maiden. Weary and sick, her steps grew slower and slower, she breathed with difficulty, and low moans escaped from her lips. Perhaps the thought of the home and friends she had lost forever, weighed her down with despair. At last she sank to the ground in a sort of fainting-fit, and refused to go farther, beseeching her master to leave her there to die; but he, unwilling to lose her, tried entreaties, then threats, and finally resorted to blows. At this juncture a lieutenant of the line came along, and hearing the cries of the poor girl inquired concerning the matter. The slave-master stated the case, on which the officer advised taking her to a physician. The other scorned the idea, but told the lieutenant he could have her for nothing, if he would take charge of her. "No," was the reply; "I will pay you three hundred piasters, otherwise when she is well you will claim her from me again."

The money was paid over, a porter carried the sufferer to the house of her new master, a physician was called, and the officer's wife, who seems to have been a benevolent woman, did all in her power to restore the invalid to health. Her efforts were attended with success, and when Spring returned with its delicious air, roses once more bloomed on the cheeks of the sick one, her eyes glanced again with their wonted fire, and she appeared to view a woman of extraordinary beauty. At this time it happened that a Pashâ, high in office, sent out his emissaries in search of another odalisque for his harém. Rumor whispered to them of the rare loveliness of our heroine, and they entered into negotiations with her master, the lieutenant, which resulted in her transfer to the Pashâ for ten thousand piasters. Her numerous graces made her at once his favorite, and all the luxuries and jewels she could desire were at her disposal.

But in her hour of prosperity, gratitude still held a place in her heart. One day, having procured a captain's commission and collected a quantity of gems and gold, she ordered out her coach and drove to the humble dwelling of the lieutenant, her former master. Alighting and entering, she presented him with the commission and gifts she had brought, exclaiming with emotion, "You saved my life, and to you I owe my prosperity; God alone can reward you for your kindness to the stranger, but these trifles will show you that I do not forget all that you have done for me."

At Samsûne, on the Euxine, a crowd of Circassian emigrants were collected on the shore to be carried in Turkish transports to various parts of the Empire. In the confusion that ensued, families were divided and separated forever. One family consisting of a man, his wife, and two children, were thus disunited, he being placed in the hold of a ship going to the Archipelago, and they being borne in another vessel to Varna, in European Turkey. From month to month she and her little boy and girl, destitute and ignorant of the language, wandered on foot towards Constantinople, where, she was informed, there were many of her countrymen, and possibly her husband might be among them. Led by this illusory hope, she at last reached the vast metropolis, and after a long search, concluded to cross over into

Asia Minor, and look for him there. In the meanwhile he had been slowly and wearily searching for his family in Asia Minor, gradually approaching Constantinople with the faint hope of meeting them somewhere within its walls. Reaching Scutari, he crossed over to Stambûl, and bewildered by the hurrying throngs, in which he was jostled hither and thither, found himself at last in a mosque court, where they were holding a weekly fair under the trees. There in the crowd he caught a glimpse of a woman having a little boy clinging to her skirts, and bearing a flaxen-haired little girl on her shoulder. With a sudden hope he followed them, and found that they were indeed his long-lost wife and children. The recital of such incidents might be multiplied to an indefinite extent, nor are surprising vicissitudes of fortune confined to the Circassian emigrés. Two of the highest officers of the realm are in the habit of joking each other on their origin, the one saying to the other, "You are not worth as much as I am, you only cost four thousand piasters, but it took five thousand piasters to buy me." They were white captives of war, and had by shrewdness and talent risen to high rank, as has been the case with most of the Grand Viziers. A negro slave has been known to become High Admiral of the Turkish navy. In Turkey the ridiculous fiction invented and fostered for political capital in the United States concerning the existence of a natural antipathy between the Black and the White races is unknown.

Will the reader be wearied by one more incident illustrative of the romance of life in Constantinople? A daughter of the late Sultan Abdûl Medjíd, and niece of the reigning Sultan, was betrothed to one of the first Pashâs of the realm, — of course in the royal as well as Oriental mode, without consulting her inclinations on the subject. But having one day caught a glimpse of her betrothed through her lattice as he rode by on his Arab barb, she chose to take umbrage at his portly form, and flatly declared that she would not have him, or rather that he should not have her. Expostulation and entreaty were alike useless to turn the haughty beauty from her resolution, in which she was strengthened by an incident that occurred a few days later. As she was out riding in the suburbs, she chanced to meet a youth whose handsome features and graceful person attracted her attention. Immediately "a spark of fine love struck upon her heart," as Froissart says of Edward III., and she bade her attendant eunuch inquire his name. He proved to be the son of a poor officer, a youth whom we shall call Areef, whose only patrimony was his good looks, an adventurer waiting for something to turn up, an Oriental Micawber, whose days were spent in smoking, dreaming over the "Loves of Leila and Medgnoon," in well-thumbed MSS., and keeping questionable company.

Bringing the same will to her aid which had induced her to reject her former suitor and which she inherited from her royal ancestors, the young Sultana resolved that Areef and none other should be her husband. By such weapons in the art of persuasion as are best known to the female mind, she overcame the opposition of her queen-mother to so preposterous an alliance, and intrigue and gold gained compliance in other quarters.

All this time Areef Effendi was idling in the coffee-shops, ignorant of the elevation that was preparing for him. But Destiny had booked him through on the express train to the Fortunate Isles, and the hour to start had come. While nodding over his narghilé, an officer in livery touched him on the shoulder: "God be praised! O Areef, we have found thee at last; come, you are wanted; a certain Sultana has sent us."

Although the impersonation of laziness, Areef was no fool. Familiar with the turns of fortune so frequent in the East, he saw at once that he "had struck a vein," and obeyed all directions without a moment's hesitation. He was taken to a bath, and thence to a tailor's, where he was clothed in a new suit; thus equipped he was conducted to a palace situated on the Bosphorus, and was left alone in a spacious hall, whose sumptuous decorations fed his fancy, while the lapping of the waves below and the perfume of jasmines and roses lulled his senses, until the merry sound of female voices whispering behind a lattice that overlooked the hall, informed him that he was undergoing inspection. After an hour he was removed, and some days later received a formal offer of the hand of the sultana. Very naturally, he accepted the proposal, but to the question, as to how he should provide the indispensable bridal presents, backsheesh to a host of menials, and an outfit for himself, he received answer not to be troubled; if Fate had destined him to be married, the necessary paraphernalia would not be wanting, and so it proved. The queen-mother furnished him with all these, and he in turn presented them to the bride and her slaves. At the threshold of matrimony we leave our friend Areef in the hands of the beneficent Fates, who have made him one of their favorites. While others toil a life-time in vain to win coy Fortune to their side, she came to him unbidden, and showered him with pearls.

III.

THE BOSPHORUS.

KEF: this is a word in the dialect of the Constantinopolitan which contains in itself the key to life, character and scenery on the Bosphorus, and, in fact, throughout Turkey. *Dolce far niente* say the Italians for nearly the same thing, in three words; the Turk has it in one syllable. So far as we know, there is no synonym for it in the English language; such inane Saxonisms as indolence and idleness are nearest to it, and they have not an honorable meaning. Tennyson's "Lotus Eaters" is the best definition of the word *Kef* to be found in our tongue; the diligent perusal of that poem will in a measure prepare the mind to comprehend the nature of life on the Bosphorus, and a few weeks or months spent in a spirit passive to the influence of its charms and devoted to a judicious course of day-dreaming under its pines and plane-trees, on its breezy heights and in its delicious vales, will afford the best translation of the word *Kef* which we can suggest.

In the following pages we can do no more than to introduce the reader to this lovely region, hoping that he may taste "the sober certainty of waking bliss" on those shores where, "if there be an Elysium on earth, it is there."

In respect to temperature, the Bosphorus is very advantageously situated. "It is the quality o' the climate" to be of a more reasonable sort than is common in this world of great heat and cold. In winter the "sweet south" from the Marmora will often soften the air and prevent very severe cold, a few blustering days of snow, and considerable raw, wet weather for a couple of months, being usually the worst that happens. During the winter of 1865 and 1866, a little milder than the average, the mercury did not descend below freezing point under cover. There were many days in mid-winter when one could sit by the water-side for hours without feeling chilly. In summer time, on the other hand, the north breezes from the Euxine cool the air and render it much more refreshing than the atmosphere of the same latitudes elsewhere. Such spasms of excessive heat as occur every summer in the United States or as continue for whole seasons in Smyrna or Naples, are unknown at Constantinople.

The facilities for visiting the various attractions of the Bosphorus are many and the prices moderate. There are always caïques or wherries to be found at all the landings, ready to take one in any direction; there are also steamers plying at different hours of the day between the villages of the Bosphorus and the city, and good riding horses and talikas, or Constantinople hacks, are ever to be found in readiness; the ride up to Buyukdéré on horseback through the villages is very novel and entertaining. A railroad on the European side is talked of and will soon be undertaken, if not already commenced. This will do very well for those doing business in Constantinople, but is otherwise not at all to our taste; and yet, while viewing with regret these innovations that seem so unsuited to the people and scenery, and give a shock to our sensibilities, we cannot help coinciding with Wordsworth when he says: —

> "Motions and Means on land and sea at war
> With old poetic feeling, not for this
> Shall ye, by Poets even, be judged amiss!
> Nor shall your presence, howsoe'er it mar
> The loveliness of Nature, prove a bar
> To the Mind's gaining that prophetic sense
> Of future change, that point of vision whence
> May be discovered what in soul ye are."

Friday is the great day of the Bosphorus;

it is the Mussulman's Sabbath, and the occasion is improved by the dwellers on the Bosphorus in "*making kef*" to their utmost ability. The beautiful valleys of Tokát, Sulymánié, Baltalimán and Geurk Soo, and the well-shaded precincts of the mosque of Beyler Béy, are the chief resorts. Thither, on pleasant days, one may see caïques speeding over the water like flocks of waterfowl, bearing festive groups in gala attire. Under the magnificent plane-trees that overhang the marge or spread their long arms over the plain, the people sit on carpets laid on the sward, which looks like a mosaic of green and gold where the rays of the sun steal through crevices in the roof of verdure and interweave with the grasses of Spring. Venders of fruit, confectionery, coffee and sherbét are patronized alike by young and old, by the laughing damsel and the gray-beard sage in flowing robes; while children dart about busy at their sports, their long hair falling around their shoulders in many-plaited braids, and bands of strolling musicians fill the air with wild and plaintive strains. To the ear that is accustomed to the exalted symphonies and intricate variations of European music, the Oriental musician must seem, in the words of Saadee, so unmelodious "that the sound of his bow would break the arteries, and his voice is more horrid than the lamentations of a man for the death of his father." But this sort of music is suited to the countries where it originated. The quick, sharp notes that die away into a prolonged elegiac monotone, then burst out again like the half-frenzied joys of a Bacchante, and float away again into a low, lingering cadence like the lament of a despairing lover, or the mournful reflections of one who has exhausted the delights of mortal existence and found them vanity, are but the expression in sound of the character of life in the East, now raging with gusts of passion that convulse the soul with the fierce raptures of love and jealousy, hate and desire, and now subsiding into long intervals of reaction, of listless, uneventful, voluptuous repose. Such, too, has been the way in which the nations of the Orient have risen and disappeared; now, inspired by visions of hoories in Paradise, they have hurled themselves with resistless energy against the bulwarks of Christendom, then they have sunk into protracted periods of enervating inaction, and, like the dying notes of their native song, have passed away from earth. There is certainly something very peculiar in the effect produced by Oriental music, even on the ear of the foreigner who listens impatiently to its strains. It does not soothe, perhaps it fails to please, and yet it agitates the listener, arouses his emotions, and fires his blood.

At these and other places of resort one may also sometimes see jugglers, the *Kara geuz* or low puppet-shows of Constantinople, dancing bears, the significant but too suggestive dances of the East, and other characteristic sights. The variety of costume and scenery to be seen combined at these concourses of the Constantinopolitans, affords subjects for the canvas which have been strangely neglected by men of genius. It is a matter of surprise and regret that artists do not visit Constantinople to find material for their pencils. It is ever to Italy and Rome that they gravitate, and we have had Italian contadinas and Neapolitan lugboats and fishermen until the subject has become conventional and almost wearisome; not that these are not in the highest degree pleasing and picturesque and suitable to transfer to canvas, but sameness and mannerism pall on the intellectual taste, and variety is agreeable even in matters intrinsically beautiful and attractive. This is a truth so well acknowledged that we should be ashamed to repeat it if it had not in reality become so trite as almost to be in danger of being forgotten by the artist of our day. At Constantinople the genre, the landscape, and the marine painter will find a virgin field and ample scope for the exercise of his powers. Does he seek for groups, what more interesting subject can he find than a band of brigand-like Bashi Bozooks or Albanians with their curious, richly mounted weapons, and their manly figures clad in the brilliant garb of Asia Minor, or the red cap, the kilt and embroidered buskins of Romélia? A cluster of women and children shopping in the bazaars, a Pashâ mounted on a Persian steed and preceded and followed by outriders, making way through a narrow street overhung by houses quaint and old as the houses of Nuremburg; an improvisatore reciting the Arabian Nights in a coffee-shop, or a group of boatmen and caïques at the foot of the grand mosque of Yení Jamee; such are a few of the thousand and one subjects that would make the fame of a genre painter. Does the artist seek for landscapes suitable for his pencil? He will find on the Bosphorus skies not inferior to the skies of Italy, sunsets as superb, sunrises as glorious, and views that have not their match elsewhere. The Rhine, the Danube, the Hudson, present in a diluted form beauties of scenery which on the Bosphorus are contained within the space of sixteen miles; nor has any one of those rivers that shifting and endless succession of varying pictures, that perfect combination of sublimity and loveliness, of softness of atmospheric tints and grandeur of outline, of art and nature, such as renders the Bosphorus the most beautiful spot on the globe. As if this were not enough, the seven hills of Constantinople, studded with gilded domes and minarets, add to most of the landscapes of the Bosphorus an element of splendor that is unique and indescribable.

Is our artist in search of subjects to match the feluccas of Genoa, he will find nothing more picturesque in the way of marine architecture than the high-prowed and high-sterned checkdemés and sakolévas that glide down the Bosphorus, lighting its blue waters with their snowy and oddly-fashioned sails; and to seize the graceful outline of the Constantinople wherries or caïques will require all his skill. They are unique of their kind; long and very narrow, tapering to a point at each end, decked at the stem and stern, with the greatest beam abaft the midships, with a very small keel, and standing considerably above the water, they are fleet as the wind, and graceful as a swan in their motion, but they require to be managed with as much steadiness as a birch-bark canoe. They are constructed of light materials, painted black, but ornamented with gilt carvings, and are rowed by one or more boatmen dressed in white, with flowing sleeves, and the invariable fez or red skull-cap of the Levant; the Sultan's caïque, which is white and profusely gilded, is rowed by twenty-six picked oarsmen. The passenger sits on ample cushions in the bottom of the boat. Nothing can be conceived more luxurious than thus reclining with one or two congenial friends, and provided with a supply of Turkish tobacco and confections, to glide hour after hour along the shores of the Bosphorus on a pleasant morning, when the water is like glass, and the palaces, the terraced gardens, the kiôsks, the old castles and the majestic groves of cypress are reflected on its tranquil bosom, while the ships swing idly at their moorings, and perhaps from the distance as from an enchanted shore, the notes of music are borne on the stilly air.

As the eye wanders languidly from one scene to another, there is scarce an object that does not recall some memory of the past, some name or action glorious in legend or history. Where the waters shimmer between Scutari and Stambûl, was fought in 1352 the great naval battle between the fleets of Venice and Genoa, commanded by Pisani and Doria, when tempestuous winds shrieked down the strait and the walls of Byzantium were lined with spectators. Where yonder dome and minaret peep above the plane and cypress trees that overshadow them, is the tomb of the great rover Haïreddeen, usually called Barbarossa, Turkey's greatest admiral, whose victorious galleys swept the Mediterranean. The white tower that near the lovely village of Bebék rises high above the wild cypresses that cluster around its base, marks the spot where Darius, going against the Scythians, crossed on a bridge of boats in the narrowest part of the Bosphorus; there also Mahomet the Second crossed two thousand years later and built that tower and the singular fortress to which it belongs, opposite to the Anadolee Hissár constructed by his father; he thus gained command of the Bosphorus preparatory to the capture of Constantinople.

But for historic associations combined with the charms of a noble prospect, commend me to the Byzantine Castle, situated on a lofty eminence named by the ancients Hierón, between the Black Sea and the mountain called the

Giant's Grave, and opposite to the corresponding height on the European side, where once existed a temple of Serapis and a castle. The Greeks and the Genoese here received toll from passing vessels, and in time of wàr stretched a boom across the strait. In the ninth century Haroon al Rescheed of glorious memory, laid siege to the fortress of Hierón after the capture of Heraklea with a force of two hundred thousand men. He raised a mound against the walls two thirds of their height, on which to place his engines, and the castle would soon have fallen if Nikephoros the Emperor had not come to terms. A large part of the mound remained untouched until within a few years, when Dr. Millingen, son of the English antiquarian of that name, once physician to Lord Byron, and now for many years attached to the royal household, and whose life has been in itself a romance, commenced investigating the castle, and began by cutting through this mound at considerable expense. The earth he found full of human bones, and after some work he reached the gate of the castle, which had been walled up during the siege; the passage for the portcullis, and the lintel and posts of the outer entrance, remained in excellent preservation; they proved to be of fine white marble, elaborately embossed with carvings such as adorn the entablatures of Greek temples. On further investigation it was discovered that in addition to these fragments, a large part of the masonry incorporated into the walls of the castle was taken from the ruins of the temple of Jupiter Urius, which occupied the site of the fortress several centuries before Christ, and was erected on the spot, where, as the legend goes, Jason consulted the oracle before launching out on the mysterious perils of the unexplored Euxine. Whatever credence may be given to the particular form of the legend, the existence of such a tradition proves that this site was employed in some way, perhaps as a beacon and a height from whence to observe changes in the weather at least three thousand years ago. Since that remote period, the Greek colonist, the Persian, the Roman, the Byzantine, the Genoese, and the Turk, have successively trod as masters on these marbles that Time has spared for our contemplation in the nineteenth century, and hung with a drapery of perennial verdure. Under the water at the foot of the height of Hierón, some fishermen discovered a marble bas-relief representing the ancient ceremony of divination for the sick. It is interesting, both as a work of art, and as illustrating the customs of antiquity. It is now in the possession of Dr. Millingen.

I visited the ruin several times, and what a grand spot it is for a prospect. With some difficulty we scaled the ivied towers, and from the ragged, storm-beaten battlements in whose crannies the sea-mew builds her nest, we saw the mouth of the Bosphorus and the Black Sea beyond, gleaming with white sails, and vast and glorious in its hues of green, purple, and blue, and with a line of foam where the breakers rushed in upon the iron shores. On turning in the opposite direction, the Bosphorus lay before us, winding from point to point, until it reached Constantinople and the Sea of Marmora, and lined with villages and kiôsks, minarets and majestic groves of pine. To add to the splendor of the prospect, the eye of imagination could see the glittering legions of Constantine the Great crossing the strait at the foot of the hill on which the castle is situated, on their way to the overthrow of Licinius; many centuries earlier, Darius stood on the same eminence, gazing on the stormy Euxine before he set out on his ill-starred expedition against the Scythians.

The great human family is framed like the

globe; as the strata of the everlasting hills are laid one on the other through long ages, so nations are founded on each other's ruin. They contribute their part in the plan of the universe, succeeding generations build upon their bones, and the mightiest empire is but a grain of sand upon the sea-shore compared with the existence of the Eternal.

The last time I visited the old castle was on a squally March afternoon in company with two English residents and a young German painter who is destined to achieve celebrity. A one-eyed, pock-marked veteran, health officer and commander of the port of Kavák, who had fought in the Greek Revolution, the Egyptian Rebellion, and the Crimea, took us over from Buyûkdéré to the Asiatic shore in his boat. We landed at Anadolee Kavák, a quaint Turkish village, much frequented by Turkish skippers, and showing few traces of Christian civilization. It is rarely troubled by the presence of travellers, who do not often go out of the beaten path to see localities not laid down in the guide-book. Here we of course stopped at the village coffee-shop, which is shaded by several fine plane-trees, and took a flingán of coffee and a pipe, after which we picked our way up to the castle, and sketched some of its prominent features, but before we could complete our task, the rain began to pour, and drove us to seek shelter in Kavák. By a singular coincidence we soon found ourselves again comfortably ensconced on the diván of the coffee-shop, each supplied with a cup of coffee, and meditatively inhaling the grateful perfumes of the narghilé. Before this interesting scene was over, we were joined by a young Greek from the Health-office, who proposed after a while that we adjourn to the Guard-house. There we were cordially received by our one-eyed friend, and, reclining on his diván, were treated by him to coffee and pipes, while he spun unconscionable yarns, and the Greek thrummed his guitar, and sung love-songs. In the meantime the storm was increasing in violence, the rain fell in torrents, the lightning flashed vividly around us, and the thunder crashed among the echoing shores of the Bosphorus. It appeared as if we might have to pass the night there, but in the evening the clouds rolled away, and after many words, without which nothing can be done in the East, we found a boatman, willing to row us over to Buyûkdéré in a caïque, drenched with water, and sufficiently overloaded to make it pleasant to step on shore again.

We entered a Greek mehané or wine-shop, to refresh ourselves, but, as it was Lent and rather late, we could only sup on meagre Lenten fare. While we were discussing our supper it was remarked that the boniface was evidently preparing to charge us a good price, as he probably did not often entertain foreigners. After we had finished, we called for the bill.

"Thirty piasters, gentlemen."

"What, sirrah! if we were natives, would you charge us more than ten piasters; and how dare you ask such a ridiculous sum of us?"

"Very true," shrugging his shoulders deprecatingly; "but you are Englishmen, and have money, and can pay reasonably for what you have."

The impudence and frankness of the varlet were so delightful, that we simultaneously burst into a long roar of laughter; when we could recover ourselves, we gave him ten piasters, and moved towards the door. He dashed the money down, tore off his fez and also flung it on the floor, and began to gesticulate, and swear by the Virgin and all the saints, that he had a sick wife, and half-a-dozen children, and that it would ruin him to entertain foreigners at the native rates. When a Greek acts in this manner, the probability is that he has been overpaid. He followed us into the street, and tried to snatch an umbrella from one of us, and hurled a paving-stone at another of the party. A seasonable punch on the head gave him new views of the stellar creation, and so incensed him that he rushed off to the koolooque, or police office. In a few moments, four stalwart zaptiéhs took us in custody, and introduced us into their quarters, where the "chief" bid us welcome, and requested us to be seated. Each party then made a statement of the case. While our side was presenting its view of the question, the bonifice repeatedly and violently interrupted us, for which he received a blow on the mouth, and a "sûs ganûm," — *anglice*, hold your tongue.

After the whole "case was in," the various items were calculated on the slates, and "the chief" looked at us deliberately before giving his decision. The result of his observation led him to the conclusion that he could not safely trifle with us, and he gave his judgment accordingly. We were to pay the plaintiff the nominal sum of twenty paras, in addition to the ten piasters we had offered him. Apparently we had lost the case, but in Turkey the winner generally pays the costs, and while the Greek got half a piaster more than we first offered him, he had to pay five or six piasters, by way of costs or backsheesh, and lost more than he gained. We lost the case, but made money by doing so; he won the case, but thereby lost money; it was like the little joker, now you see it, and now you don't. Was not that a judgment worthy of Solomon?

The village of Buyûkdéré, where this little incident occurred, is one of the most charming of the many delightful locations of the Bosphorus; it is situated for the most part on one side of a broad promenade, by the water's edge, and contains many sumptuous residences, among others the summer resorts of most of the foreign embassies. In the evening, when the moon rises in her glory above the hills, and silvers the rippling waters of the Bosphorus, the quay is alive with ladies and gentlemen, and a band of music blends its mellow strains with the trill of the nightingale.

Near the village is the famous plane-tree under which Godfrey de Bouillon is said to have encamped. The tree is certainly very large and venerable, but whether it is seven hundred years old or not is very doubtful. There is also good reason to believe that Godfrey de Bouillon and his hosts never visited this spot.

The following morning I returned to Bebék, a quiet little village, about five miles from the city. Like most of the villages of the Bosphorus, it is built in a hollow, the houses rising one above the other, on terraces along the very steep hill-sides, and looking as if they were about to topple over upon each other. At first sight, one is at a loss to imagine how these houses are to be reached, but on further acquaintance with the place, all sorts of curious, winding, narrow, and precipitous lanes are discovered, up which one picks his way slowly, stopping often to look back on the glimpses of the water that reveal themselves at every turn. On a sudden, a door seems to stop further progress, and on entering one is ushered into a spacious house with high and airy apartments, around which divans invite to recline by the windows and revel in the prospects unfolded to view. The terrace on which the house stands is seen immediately below, with its orange, and laurel, and pomegranate trees; lower still another terrace and its house and garden, and below that the main street of the village. The same scene seems to be repeated on the opposite side of the narrow gorge, and, as if framed like a picture, beyond and between the hills lies the Bay of Bebék, the valley of

Geurk Soo, or the Heavenly Waters, and the white tower mounting guard over the strait. As you sit by the open window, the breeze from the sea wafts in the fragrance of roses and the low monotone of the pines that seem with their dreamy and perpetual music to chant the mysterious march of the passing years.

The mall of Bebék is by the waterside, and is shaded by a group of majestic plane-trees. There the villagers gather at all hours of the day, particularly towards evening, and take their coffee and smoke their narghilés. A good part of my last visit to Constantinople was passed in that delicious spot, beautiful in itself, but rendered still more attractive by the many associations that have hallowed it. There the hours of the past would again return, and for a while I could almost forget that youth and its joyance once gone are gone forever. It is the glory of that climate, that one may sit out of doors the greater part of the year without inconvenience.

A coffee-shop in Kutchûk, or Little Bebék, was one of my favorite haunts of a morning. There the fishermen could be seen drying or mending their nets, under the shade of the chenars, or watching for fish from their quaint fishing houses, perched high in air, or pitching their boats on the beach. A group of peasants, a knot of Turkish women and children, or a horse laden with panniers of oranges and grapes, would happen along to help fill up the picture, while the ever-present Bosphorus stretched away in the distance, — purple hillsides gleaming through the golden haze of morn.

To the foreigner, Bebêk offers unusual attractions, as being in a sense almost a colony of English, Americans, and Germans. Its vicinity to Constantinople and its healthy and agreeable location, render it a desirable residence for both merchant and missionary, and accordingly a number of Protestant families are to be found here, forming a delightful little coterie, harmoniously united by kindred tastes and interests. In that quiet, unpretending little village, one may enjoy the society of men of commanding genius, whose life experience has abounded in rare and stirring incident, and whose various talents have been devoted to the reformation of a vast empire; there books have been translated, and youth have been educated whose influence for good will be more and more evident as the ages go by. Dr. Schauffler, well known for his singular career, his earnestness as a missionary, and his great powers as a linguist, a preacher, a musician, and a conversationalist, has resided for the last eighteen or twenty years in Bebék. The seminaries of the American Board, which were established there, are now located in the interior, but the College founded by Mr. Robert is now situated there, and, as is well known, is under the able charge of Dr. Hamlin. It seems to be fairly under way, and promises to become a powerful agent in the advancement of education in Turkey. It is difficult for Americans to understand what a soul-trying work it is to start such an institution in the East, and in fact any thing that savors in the least degree of progress and reform. The College now occupies the large and imposing building formerly the seat of the Armenian Seminary. It was originally the residence of a wealthy Armenian, who built it many years ago. In those turbulent times, when the Janizaries were a terror to the Christians, and even menaced the throne itself, the owner kept his house rusty and black on the exterior, in order to avert suspicion of the wealth he had accumulated within its spacious halls, — a frequent device in those days; but this did not save him; the Janizaries marked him for their own, and on three successive occasions they sacked the house and threatened the life of their helpless and unoffending victim.

Opposite Bebék, where the Bosphorus is the narrowest, is the village of Kandillee, clinging to the steep sides of a promontory, that stands boldly out into the stream, and is bathed by the dashing waters of the rapid current that flings a diamond spray to the sunlight and murmurs a perpetual music as it rushes by the kiosks that line the shores. The prospect from the brow of the eminence is perhaps the most magnificent of all the many marvellous views which the Bosphorus presents. Reclining in a window, one may gaze on one hand up to the Black Sea, with the grand old castles of Europe and Asia in the foreground below; then, turning in the opposite direction, the eye may follow the devious strait bordered with lovely villages and palaces until it rests on the Sea of Marmora, and the glittering spires of Constantinople. If the traveller has but a short time to spend in Constantinople, and would desire to obtain the best idea of the scenery of the Bosphorus attainable from one spot, we strongly advise him to row up to Kandillee in a caïque, on some pleasant morning, and climbing up its steep but very clean streets, make his way to a half-finished and unoccupied palace on the summit, so conspicuous as to be easily found. There, seated under the columns of the marble portico, he may spend hours undisturbed in the contemplation of one of the most superb and impressive scenes which it is given to mortal man to behold this side of Paradise. The wondrous associations of antiquity, the monuments of past ages, the grandeur and loveliness of Nature, the delicacy of climate, and the softness of atmospheric tints that invest every object with magic hues, are here combined in a perfection that may be equalled, but cannot be elsewhere surpassed. The prospect from the steps of the Parthenon over the Acropolis, the plain of Athens, its amphitheatre of historic mountains, and the white-sailed Egean beyond, and the view from Kandillee described above, may be considered as presenting the most inspiring and suggestive spectacles in Greece and Turkey.

IV.

ISLAM.

TOWARD the last of November the great annual pilgrimage of the faithful started from Constantinople for Mecca. The sacred camels adorned with green and gold trappings, were loaded with the votive offerings of the Sultan, at the palace of Beshiktâsh, where he now resides; they were then ferried over to Scutary, on the opposite shore of the Bosphorus, with a considerable number of pilgrims, after receiving the blessing of the Shekh ul Islám, and started for the long journey to the shrine of the Prophet, from which so few live to return. The whole pilgrimage was formerly accomplished by land, but now steamers share with the ships of the desert the privilege of transporting the deluded multitude of fanatics to their destination. Strange and thrilling incidents have sometimes occurred on board these pilgrim-laden vessels. Years ago the Austrian steamer *Stambûl*, on the voyage succeeding the one that took me to Trebizond, carried a deck-load of the pious to Constantinople. On the trip the fanatics arose against the crew of Infidels, and before they could be got under, the captain and several of his men were killed.

It was on the Brenda, two years ago, I think, that a similar catastrophe was very near occurring. Several hundred pilgrims embarked on her, but as they went on board, instead of being disarmed, as is generally the rule, they were carelessly allowed to retain their long yataghans and muskets. Their shekh, a bloodthirsty fanatic, took the opportunity when the captain was on the bridge conning the vessel, to get him into his power, after which they mastered and prepared to massacre the crew. But the chief engineer, a canny Scotchman, hearing a commotion on deck, looked through the skylight, and divined the state of affairs at a glance. His ready wit suggested the novel expedient of scalding the ruffians with boiling water through the hose. Disconcerted and overcome by this unforeseen enemy in the rear, the pilgrims surrendered at discretion, and were deprived of the means of creating further mischief.

The last terrible visitation of the cholera seems to have been clearly traced to Mecca, or rather to Jedda, its seaport, where vast numbers of pilgrims were collected at the time when the annual festival of Korbán Bairám required the sacrifice of very many thousands of sheep. The refuse of the slaughter was culpably allowed by the Pashâ of the district to putrefy, the air became immediately tainted, and enormous multitudes were swept into eternity within a few days. From Jedda, the disease was carried to Suez and Alexandria. From Alexandria the scourge came to Constantinople in a Turkish frigate, whose officers infamously escaped quarantine, by taking false oaths. The knave of a port physician who, it is said, was bribed to give them pratique, was decapitated, but this did not prevent the epidemic from spreading through the narrow streets of the capital, like a fire on a western prairie. For six weeks the angel of death knocked at the doors of the doomed. Of the inmates of forty houses standing in a row, all but thirty died in one night. The malignity of the disease exceeded any thing known in its previous appearance in those parts, and the number of deaths soon rose to over a thousand a day. The panic among the inhabitants now became something frightful. While thousands were hurried uncoffined to the crowded cemeteries, thousands of the living, unmindful of their duty to their dying friends, fled to the Black Sea in overloaded boats, or encamped on the hills outside of the city, often with scarce a rag to shelter them from the sun and rain. This alone created much suffering. With energy rather unusual in Turkey, a medical board of supervision was established by the government which did a little toward alleviating the horrors of the occasion. None were more indefatigable or successful in their labors at this awful time than the missionaries. Day and night they were engaged in their labors of mercy, and out of the many cases they treated they lost less than fourteen per cent. The remedy they chiefly employed was the famous Hamlin mixture, familiar to the profession, together with unremitting watchfulness in diet, and the use of restoratives and external applications, the great secret of success in many cases being the use of the mixture on the first appearance of diarrhœa, which most frequently is the premonitory symptom of an attack. It is easy for medical men to make light of the remedy employed, but facts are stubborn things, the statements of the missionaries are beyond question, and until the faculty can discover some treatment of this terrible disease that can save more than *eighty-six per cent. of all cases,* they do themselves little credit in decrying the treatment to which we have alluded.

The number of victims was variously estimated, but, from the burial teskerés or licenses granted during the prevalence of the epidemic and other data, we are inclined to think that little less than fifty thousand perished during the six weeks of its continuance. The plague of 1837 carried off one hundred and seven thousand persons, but it lingered for nearly a year.

Some of the non-Protestant Bulgarians of Constantinople, who were moved with gratitude for the attentions the missionaries had bestowed on them and their countrymen during the pestilence, presented them with an address of thanks. This was the more pleasing because gratitude is not one of the prominent virtues of the Oriental Christian, being sufficiently rare to excite surprise when exhibited. In passing we may observe that the Bulgarians are perhaps the most promising of the many races under the Ottoman dominion,—the Armenians ranking next in hopeful characteristics. Less vivacious, acute, versatile, and handsome than the Greeks, they however display more uniform self-respect, common sense, and sincerity. A strong desire for independence and thirst after progress and knowledge, are gradually preparing the Bulgarians for the day when they shall be finally emancipated from the Turkish rule.

Late in February occurred the great week of the Turkish year, answering to the Holy Week of the Romish Church; as the Turkish months are lunar, this event varies from year to year in the season of its arrival. In this instance the week began on February 20th, which was the anniversary of the period when Mohammed first experienced the divine inspirations that resulted in the Koran. In celebration of this event, the Sultan repaired in the evening to the elegant mosque of Tôpe Hané. Most of the Ottoman fleet had been brought out of their winter quarters in the Golden Horn and moored in the Bosphorus, in anticipation of the occasion. As night came on illuminations became visible from shore to shore; the men-of-war were lighted up with battle-lanterns from stem to stern, from deck to masthead, and the mosque of Tôpe Hané and its pair of lofty and graceful minarets were a blaze of glory; when the Sultan set out from his palace the artillery of frigates and line-of-battle ships rent the air with long-reverberating peals that rumbled up the steep, winding shores of the Bosphorus like a thunder-storm in mountain gorges; then fireworks were sent into the sky, and night was turned into day. After this spectacle was over every Mussulman was in anxious expectation for the appearance of the new moon, that would close the annual fast of Ramazán and inaugurate the Baïrâm or three days' jubilee. Every Mohammedan considers himself a special watchman appointed to discover the new moon at this time, and couriers or telegrams are sent from different quarters where it has been visible to the naked eye; so that if clouds should interfere with its appearance at the capital, Baïrâm can still begin.

As soon as the intelligence of the moon's discovery is known, salvos of artillery are fired, and on the ensuing morning the Sultan gives his great annual reception, in the precincts of the Seraglio, to the "lords spiritual and temporal" of the empire. At sunrise he goes to one of the chief mosques and offers his devotions, and then returns to the Seraglio to hold his levee. The *corps diplomatique* have a gallery from whence to witness the ceremony, and are expected to attend. Four or five tickets admitting each a gentleman and lady, are sent to each of the embassies for distribution to friends or travellers. I was so fortunate as to have a ticket placed at my disposal, and had a fine opportunity of observing all that was to be seen. A merry company of six, we left the village of Bebék on the Bosphorus at daybreak, in a comfortable caïque, and reached Stambûl in season to see the royal procession going and returning from the mosque of Achmét. The royal band struck up the "Carvinal at Venice" and other familiar airs; then, through a lane of soldiers in sumptuous uniforms, came the generals and other public men of the empire, dressed in a style magnificent beyond description, and mounted on Arab horses caparisoned with equal splendor, and beautiful as any steeds that ever trod the earth. Such a display of sleek, graceful, spirited, thoroughbred animals is seen but rarely in a lifetime. Last of all came Fuâd Pashâ, the Grand Vizíer, after whom followed the royal body-guard, magnificently uniformed and composed of as handsome a collection of men as could be found anywhere; many of them are over six feet, and few are under that height. A curious feature of the guard is a mounted company composed of the scions of families of rank representing the various races under the Ottoman dominion, two from each race, in the peculiar costume of their respective nationalities, and riding their steeds like centaurs. After these came the Sultan, Abdûl Azíz, in plain black; then followed several regiments of cavalry, and lastly a confused multitude of spectators.

We presented our tickets at the gate of the Seraglio, and on securing our position, saw the Sultan under one of the broad-roofed, gayly decked porticoes so characteristic of the Seraglio, and of Constantinople. He was seated on a golden throne placed on a heavy, embroidered carpet of crimson satin. Then the Grand Vizíer approached and kissed the hem of the carpet, and was followed in succession by the different pashas according to rank; these were succeeded by the Shekh ul Islám, the high-priest of Mohammedanism and the expounder of its laws, — a fine, venerable man, supported by two attendants; the Sultan stood up to receive him; then came a long train of inferior priests, clad in green and purple tunics massively embroidered with gold. During the whole of this ceremony Abdûl Azíz, except in one or two instances, received his kneeling subjects with an indifference approaching disdain, gazing around at the foreigners present, stroking his beard, and at one time actually smiling, and holding his hand over his mouth as if to restrain an impulse to laugh. As soon as the ceremony was over he rose, and reëntered the kiosk rapidly, as if he considered the whole thing a wearisome farce.

Some who have investigated the origin of this annual pageant, incline to the opinion that it is the continuation of a ceremony borrowed after the Turkish conquest from the Byzantine court, and the ceremonial of the Byzantine emperors was but the triumphs of consular and imperial Rome transferred to Constantinople and celebrated annually; so that this Turkish spectacle may be considered a sequel to a custom established rather more than two thousand years ago. Nothing equalling its barbaric splendor is to be seen anywhere else in this age. It reminds one of the marvellous tales of the "gorgeous East;" it is like a vision of the "Arabian Nights." A stranger gazing on such pomp and splendor would find it difficult to realize what poverty and wretchedness are the lot of the millions of Turkey, and on the verge of what an abyss it is tottering, were it not that the vivid contrast presented by the squalid streets, the decaying houses, the stolid throngs, along the route of the pageant, suggested the true condition of the country. It was exactly the same with the power that preceded it; long after the Eastern or Lower Empire had nothing left to it but the territory immediately around Constantinople and the meagre glory of a shadowy renown, the ceremonials and external attributes of royalty were observed as rigorously as if the Byzantine sceptre still ruled from the Euphrates to the Danube.

Such is the present condition of the Turkish monarchy. At the capital there is a certain show of splendor, but in the provinces there is grinding oppression and untold misery. The high officials put their subordinates under a force-pump, and they in turn squeeze the people. "The Devil take the hindmost" is the universal principle of action. Brigandage, misrule, peculation, starvation, ruin, and perhaps depopulation, run riot throughout the empire. The government is bankrupt; it is obliged to negotiate frequent loans at enormous discounts to meet the interest on the rapidly accumulating public debt and the expenses of the superbly uniformed guards, the iron-clads, and the women of the Sultan. When I was last in Constantinople most of the government employés had received no pay for seven months, while the Sultan made no change in his lavish expenditures, and the chief pashâs and generals took care that there should be no deficit in their salaries. It must be said, however, that even the highest dignitaries of the realm are sometimes pinched for means. Their position requires them to maintain considerable external pomp, while their private menage is often on a very reduced scale; there are few in Turkey who do not lead a sort of hand-to-mouth existence. And all this, be it remembered, is not in a young country, with an enterprising people and abundant resources like ours, that might shake off the nightmare of despair that weighs it down and start anew with renovated powers. The nation is in its dotage, and is more like some hoary sinner made prematurely decrepit by excess, than like the venerable patriarch who in a green old age is crowned with glory and honor.

The press, limited as is its influence, is subsidized to represent affairs *couleur de rose.* It is a useless task to undertake to arouse the Sultan to a knowledge of the true state of affairs in his dominions. The attempt is generally attended with the loss of favor, nor are there many found sufficiently virtuous or courageous to approach him with unpleasant information or advice. During my stay in Constantinople, one of the first pashâs of the empire ventured to enlighten Abdûl Azíz as to the state of the treasury and the corrupt practices ot Fuâd Pashâ the Grand Vizíer. The Sultan was filled with rage when the melancholy revelation disclosed to him a condition of things of which he had never dreamed. Extensive reforms in the conduct of the administration were confidently predicted as the result of these disclosures, and so certain seemed the downfall of Fuâd Pashâ that the parasites of the court already began to curry favor with his supposed successor, the pashâ who had opened the eyes of the Sultan. But Fuâd Pashâ found means to regain his influence over his royal master, who made him a gift of £10,000 at the Great Baïrám as a token of returning confidence, and the Grand Vizíer had the additional satisfaction of seeing his rival sent into a sort of honorary exile. Fuâd Pashâ is, however, no worse, but probably better than the greater part of the Turkish pashâs. He is something of a literary character, and was in early life a schoolmaster; he has also written the best existing grammar of the Turkish language. Theoretically he belongs to the party of reform, and doubtless does all he can for the progress of Turkey consistently with his own interests, but these, we fear, lead him too often out of the path of rectitude prescribed for the guidance of the pure-hearted and high-minded statesman and patriot.

It is difficult to imagine a truly able, and at the same time disinterested and faithful, man as Grand Vizíer of Turkey in these her degenerate days. Virtue has no part in the counsels of the empire. A handsome person, address, cunning, these are the passports to the places of honor in the East. Turk and Christian alike agree as to the worth of the moral qualities in the abstract, but they are also agreed in regarding them as impracticable in the conduct of life, and as but poor recommendations to their possessor. The last great statesman and patriot of Turkey was Achmét Kuprilee, who died in 1674.

Turkey as an independent power has survived so many years and generations since its fall was first predicted, that he must indeed be a bold man who will venture any more prophecies on the subject. But it requires, notwithstanding, very little penetration to perceive that the empire is only held together by the great Christian powers, and that, on the failure of any one of these supporters to prop the tottering fabric, it will crumble to pieces and be resolved into its original elements, which will either be swallowed up by Russia or be reëstablished on the national bases that existed before the Turkish invasion. In European Turkey the number of Ottomans forms so small a proportion of the whole population, — less than 1,500,000, — and the Christians of the Principalities are so vigorously arousing to a desire for their long-lost freedom, that it is difficult to see how the sway of the Crescent can continue many years longer north of the Bosphorus. The Turk in Europe has always been an exotic; but it would be a very possible thing for a diminished but more homogeneous, and therefore a reinvigorated, Ottoman monarchy to exist for some centuries yet in Asia Minor, where the Moslems are on a more congenial soil, and number nearly fifteen millions. The radical defect of the Turkish rule is that it is founded on the Koran and is essentially theocratic, and therefore, while tolerably well adapted to the age in which it originated, it contains within itself the seeds of decay. Progress is fatal to its existence. The introduction of the civil and military reforms of Europe into Turkey is a concession drawn from the weakness of a system that abhors but adopts them as a last resort, and in the vain hope that by this means the inevitable doom may be averted. Such a concession is the recent ordinance allowing the printing of the Koran for the purpose of its more general diffusion, so as to counteract the influence of the books disseminated by the missionaries; hitherto it has been held that to preserve the Koran in other than manuscript forms would be a profanation. The progress of Christianity may elevate the condition of the Turks individually, but it strikes at the very basis on which the throne of Othman is established, and seals the fall of his dynasty. It is no more than natural that Mohammedan laws should be rigorous, as they have been, against those who leave Islamism to embrace Christianity, for by so doing they abjure not only their religion, but also to a great degree their citizenship. This applies with similar force to those who forsake any of the Christian sects of the East to become Protestants, and is some slight palliation for the religious persecutions that have occurred there so frequently. In this view of the question we can somewhat understand what a decisive triumph Christianity achieved when Turkey abolished the death penalty against Mohammedans who become Christians; when the Sultan signed the edict that erased that law from the Turkish code, he signed the death-warrant of the Ottoman Empire. The demand of the Christian powers for this fatal measure was like the "habet" pronounced by the throngs of the Coliseum, which sealed the wounded gladiator's doom.

There is another cause that would alone hasten the extinction of the Turkish power. The Turks as a race are handsome and manly, and yield to none in valor; and although more cruel than most Christian nations, are naturally less sanguinary than the Persians and some other Eastern races; but there is a limit beyond which the national character finds it impossible to make further civil and political progress; and, as with some other Oriental tribes, and with the North American Indians, intercourse with superior races seems rather to degrade than to elevate. The Turks on the seaboard, for example, have, by contact with Europeans, become greatly vitiated, and present few of the lofty traits which ennobled the barbarism of their ancestors, and which are still to be found in the more secluded regions of Asia Minor. Although they have a long coast abounding in good harbors, and although they possess a territory rich in soil beyond many, yet they are neither a maritime, commercial, nor a really agricultural people by nature, and this alone would seem to insure the disappearance of the Turks as a distinct people. Nomadic in their origin, they still, after the lapse of ages, retain many of the characteristics of their sires who roamed over the steppes beyond the Oxus, and, like other pastoral races, are destined to be overcome and absorbed or swept away by the energy and intelligence of Christian civilization.

Abdûl Azíz has the reputation of being the most accomplished spendthrift of the age. Building and pulling down palaces, purchasing iron-clads that cost £500,000 each and are of no use except to amuse the warlike tastes of the Sultan, following the chase, and gliding about in his steam yachts, these are the chief occupations of the descendant of Sulymân the Magnificent and the ruler of thirty-one millions. It is easy from our advanced position to blame him; it is not so easy to give him our pity; and yet he is deserving of both. Can a man be born too late? this is a question for casuists to decide, but when we consider the fate of Abdûl Azíz, we are inclined to answer in the affirmative. He is not destitute of talents, of strength of character, of ambition, but the qualities he possesses are not such as enable him to make a figure in this age. He has inherited the inclinations of Bayazíd Ilderím and of Mahomet the Second. Had he lived in the days when the irregular soldiery and rude civilization of Christendom were on a par with the Tartar races, Abdûl Azíz might have hurled his triumphant Janizaries against the walls of Vienna, and blanched the cheek of many a Christian maiden with the terror of his name. But what can he do now with such ill-timed talents, kept in seclusion during the greater part of his life, ignorant of a system of finances and government contrary to all the traditions of his house, and conscious that inexorable Fate, that doom from which the true believer feels that there is no appeal, hangs impending over the empire bequeathed to him by his fathers? Those very pageants and lavish displays which are the chief cause of grievance against his reign, would in other days have emblazoned the pages of Turkish history with the hues of romance. Is it strange that he chafes against the customs and the laws of nations of his time, that he longs to draw his scimetar against the cross, and that he is haunted by the awful demon of melancholy when he finds himself powerless to act?

What is more sad than to see a nation gradually sinking to its grave? We may not necessarily approve its character nor desire its continued existence; but when we read upon its brow the marks of dissolution, and know that ere long a great nation must pass away forever to the halls of oblivion, we must be hard-hearted indeed not to sympathize in the agonies of the falling race. This it is which imparts such a softness, such a tender beauty, to the ruins, the monuments, the scenery, and the people of Constantinople. It is the pensive loveliness that rests upon the quiet hills in the closing days of Autumn when the year is dying — a loveliness more in harmony with the deeper emotions of the soul than the radiance of Spring. Go linger in the deserted halls of the doomed capital, glide gently by her crumbling palaces, and dream the hours away on her gray, forsaken walls, against which the wave beats unheeded, where the sea-bird dwells and the wild poppy nods in the sighing wind of the south; there ponder the fate of empires, the transitory nature of human affairs, the littleness of man, and the vastness of eternity.

V.

THE STAR IN THE EAST.

NO work that aims to give a correct view of the various social systems of Turkey, and of the diverse agencies that are agitating or overturning its institutions, can with justice avoid mention of the missions which have already produced such remarkable results, and are yet destined to revolutionize the character of Oriental organizations. It is cause for regret that so few of the many able volumes on Turkey should give only a passing notice to a question of such importance, even then too often dismissing the subject with a jest or a sneer. We have even known of clergymen who, when visiting the Levant, have been cordially and hospitably entertained by the missionaries, and have exhibited much interest in the antiquities and scenery around them, but have avoided inquiries into the missionary work or given it but a superficial glance, and on their return home have reported unfavorably on the progress of missions. Happily such extreme cases are exceptions.

In order rightly to estimate the results which missions have actually achieved, one must have a thorough acquaintance with the various races, creeds, and customs of the people whom the missionary is endeavoring to elevate; without such information he cannot fairly apprehend what should be reasonably expected from the missionary enterprise, and whether the results are equivalent to the effort expended. One must also have sufficient knowledge of the progress made by other people under similar conditions, and sufficient breadth of view to enable him to see the relations of things, to draw just analogies and to arrive at impartial conclusions. It is needless to say that many of the writers on Turkey have allowed themselves to approach the subject of missions in such a manner as to lead us to think them destitute of the above qualifications.

Although the missionaries would be the last to say it, we venture to plead in their behalf, that it is both ungenerous and unmanly to treat their endeavors with levity, even supposing them to be in a measure unsuccessful: the noble object to which their efforts are directed, the sacrifices which they have made for the cause of benevolence, and the character and talents that most of them possess, which would have enabled many of them to attain wealth, position, and fame, if they had preferred their emolument to the dictates of conscience, these alone should secure for them the respect of those who have occasion to allude to their labors, even if they consider those labors misdirected.

It is not in the scope of this little volume to give here a table of statistics on this subject, for which we refer the reader to the publications of the missionary societies, although it may be apropos in passing to remind him that less than fifty years ago there was not a missionary to any race within the vast territory of the Sultan; Christianity, except in name, had no existence; the Bible was not to be found in the vernacular tongues; to abjure Mohammedanism was certain death; and a moral apathy characterized the universal Oriental mind, which seemed effectually to hinder religious and intellectual progress for ages to come. Not half a century has elapsed, — one of the first missionaries sent out still lives, and one of the heroic pioneers, Dr. Goodell, has but recently passed away, —

and already we see stations scattered over all parts of the Turkish Empire from the Danube to the Nile, the centres of Protestant communities where missionaries are resident and churches are established, with a constantly increasing number of members, while many of the neighboring towns display a rapidly growing interest in the spread of practical Christianity. We see hundreds and thousands who, through violent persecutions, civil disabilities, and contumely, have stood firm in the faith which their conscience has accepted; we see schools where thousands of youth are preparing for future usefulness, and seminaries where pastors have been trained, who are in a large measure supported by the indigent churches over which they are installed; we see the Bible and hundreds of other volumes translated into many distinct dialects; we see the death penalty abolished, and missionaries allowed to labor among the Mohammedans unmolested; we see women learning to read and to realize that they are intellectual and responsible beings; we see the Protestants constituting a separate civil community, represented by their chosen agent or head at the Grand Porte; we see them recognized and respected by the sects which exhausted all human effort to crush the aspiring spirit of religious and civil liberty, that liberty of conscience unknown before in the East since the creation; and finally, after much tribulation, we see the Protestant a man whose rectitude is honored even by his enemies, whose word is taken as truth, and whose example many would gladly follow if they could muster the moral courage to break loose from the shackles of prejudice or worldly interest which enthrall them.

If missions in Turkey had accomplished no more than this, it would be more than sufficient to close the lips of the caviler, and they who have given their hearts, their labors, and their lives to the cause would be still entitled to the lasting gratitude of mankind. But great as are the apparent results of the missionary enterprise, greater than there was any reason to expect in so brief a period, the work yet to be accomplished is so much more vast, that if nothing more had been done, we might still feel at times a degree of impatience if this were all. But it is not all; the results we see are but the blossoms just appearing in the top of the tree, which are destined to cover every bough with beautiful flowers that will in time yield an abundant fruition. The real work which missions have wrought, and which cannot be set down in figures, but must be presented to the contemplation of the reflecting mind, is a work of preparation, of sowing the seed that shall be harvested by generations yet to be. The progress of the race to higher planes of moral and religious culture is gradual and, to our short-sighted vision, slow; "there is no being so certain as God, and none so slow." It requires little knowledge of history to perceive that the outbreak of revolutions, the upheaval of monarchies, the overthrow of tyrannical hierarchies, the transformation of the social and moral economy of communities, however sudden they may appear to the superficial observer, do in reality result from causes more or less obvious operating for ages, until affairs become ripe for the change, and reach that critical point when a seemingly trivial matter produces tremendous consequences; when the yielding of a barrier suddenly floods the country with waters that have silently accumulated until they could rend the dykes asunder. It is evident that there are laws governing the moral as well as the physical world, and the progress of missionary reform has generally conformed to these laws. This line of reasoning should by no means be understood as leading to the adoption of the fatalistic theory, that would dispense with the necessity and efficacy of the means usually employed in promoting the spiritual welfare of mankind.

From this point of view we are able to gain a correct estimate of the results which missions have actually achieved already in Turkey. Millions of volumes have been issued in many different languages and dialects, and disseminated over extensive regions; two hundred thousand copies of the Bible alone, in twenty languages, have been thus scattered over the land during the last eight years and a half, a large portion of them having been purchased by the natives out of their poverty, so great is the desire for the gospel. Thus is bread cast upon the waters which shall appear again in due time; thus the rising generations are educated and elevated, and seed is sown whose fruits shall increase more and more abundantly as the ages go by. Take, for example, the *Avedaper*, a bi-monthly newspaper in Armenian, issued at Constantinople, first proposed and started by Mr. Benjamin, after attempting for years to procure permission for its publication from the public censor. He was able to issue but two or three numbers, but since his death it has been continued by the mission. A thousand copies now find their way over all parts of the Turkish Empire. When a copy reaches a subscriber in a village remote among the mountains, he reads it to his neighbors who drop in of an evening, or it is read and discussed in the village coffee-shop, or it is borrowed by one and another, until it is worn to shreds. Mr. Bliss, the present editor, estimates that the 1000 copies subscribed for have 10,000 readers; we are inclined to think that his estimate is too low.

Here is another example of the way rays of light are gradually dispelling the moral gloom that broods over those lands. It was my privilege to be present on a certain evening at the weekly meeting held by Mr. Trowbridge, the city missionary, in one of the many khans or caravanseries in which natives visiting Constantinople for business take up their abode during their sojourn in the city. On this occasion there were fifty-three present, — Armenians, Bulgarians, Greeks, and Turks, — and they were from forty-two different towns in the Turkish Empire. Most of these men were intending to return sooner or later whence they had come; they would carry away more or less impression of the truth they have heard at those meetings, and not a few would take with them Bibles or other instructive volumes, perhaps to places far off in the interior, where the missionary had not yet penetrated. Years will elapse, and then perhaps calls for aid will suddenly come from that distant town, the missionary will visit the place and find many ready to welcome him and the truth he proclaims; and the cause of this awakening may be traced to some little tract or some suggestive words carried away, pondered, and discussed by one who has attended an evening meeting in a Constantinople khan. Similar cases have repeatedly occurred.

The question of civil and religious reform is already agitating almost all the numerous races that compose the heterogeneous empire of Turkey. Many, who are not yet willing to forsake their civil relations, are still sufficiently aroused to demand a higher order of priesthood, a purer life on the part of the clergy, and liberty for the laity to own and to read the Bible in the spoken tongues. It is not impossible that the problem of Oriental Christianity may eventually be solved in this manner; that is, that the ferment working in the Greek, the Armenian, and the Nestorian Churches may result in the thorough purification of those corrupt systems, and the reëstablishment of their influence over the people on a liberal and truly evangelical basis; although it must be confessed that it requires strong faith to foresee such a result. But when we consider what a revolution has taken place since the missionaries first went to Turkey, forty years ago, what a general commotion has succeeded the profound stupor of superstition which then oppressed Christian and Mohammedan alike, we find abundant encouragement for future effort. To go into the details of the changes in Turkey which are traceable to missions would be to write volumes; those only who have lived there many years can fully realize what has been performed, and how great is the promise for coming ages. That very sagacious writer, Defoe, remarks in Robinson Crusoe, "I have often observed that the Christian religion always civilizes and reforms their manners where it is received, whether it works saving effects upon them or no:" and this applies to Protestant missions in the East. Their influence for social reform is felt in a thousand ways, even when it only affects the temporal condition of the people. Science, commerce, increased means of intercourse, and even a higher tone of legislation, have followed in the wake of the first vessel that sailed from Boston with missionaries on board. It is proper to state that these observations are not made in the interest of any one missionary society, but apply to most of the evangelical associations laboring for the moral elevation of the Oriental races.

If the traveller in the Levant, who usually visits only Constantinople and other seaport towns of Turkey, sees less of the immediate results of missionary labors there than he expected to find, it is because the work there has more of a preparatory character than elsewhere; there is the arsenal where the weapons are prepared that are to overthrow the army of the aliens; there the Bible is translated; there books and periodicals are edited and printed, and from thence scattered throughout the Orient. It is a silent, unobtrusive work, the work of the press, but it is the mighty lever by which superstitions and tyrannies are uprooted, and by which nations are reëstablished on the lasting foundations of truth.

Another reason why Constantinople presents fewer converts in proportion to other stations is on account of the far greater degree of vice and frivolity existing in a capital of that size. A sensible man does not look for sunbeams from cucumbers, nor does he go to New York City or New Orleans to gain correct notions as to the condition of vital Christianity in the United States; no more should he look to Constantinople for the most apparent results of missionary effort in Turkey.

In a word, the trumpets have been blown around the strongholds of error; the walls are toppling to the fall. The final and overwhelming triumph of the Cross may not be in our day and generation, but it is none the less certain, although the onward march should continue down the ages of the hereafter. In the protracted struggle, prejudices and customs venerable with age may be overthrown; communities may be shaken to their foundations, and governments and empires may pass away to make room for organizations better adapted to the growing wants of progressive races; but through all these convulsions one great fact will become more and more prominent — the mental, moral, and physical condition of the people will be elevated; the burial of the corrupt systems of the East will be followed by the resurrection of the Oriental tribes to spheres of usefulness and prosperity more worthy of the immortal soul.

VI.

ANATOLIA.

EARLY in January I made a trip to Nicomedia. It is a city about fifty miles from Constantinople, once a place possessing celebrity and splendor, but now fallen from its high estate, and but rarely visited by foreigners. A deck passage on a small Turkish steamer was the mode of going thither, and one is well repaid for whatever discomforts attend travel on these Turkish boats by the beauties of the surrounding scenery, and the entertainment afforded by the amusing groups clustered on the deck, warming themselves around the funnel, or saying their prayers at noon. As we glided across the Marmora, we had the snow-clad range of the Bithynian Olympus before us, nine thousand feet high.

We touched at two or three points in the Gulf of Nicomedia, and found diversion in observing the skill of the Turkish seamen. The water was smooth as a mill-pond, but they so managed as to stave in the bulwarks at the pier of Daridgé. The captain, the mate, the pilot, the cook, the sailors, all gave orders at the same time, all shouting to the steersman different directions, and all swearing without stint. The art of swearing is carried to the highest perfection in the East. There was doubtless considerable talent of that sort developed in our army, and choice specimens may be heard at Denver and Washoe; but after all, those who cultivate the "black art" in America have much to learn before they can attain the eloquence, the volubility, the rich fancy, the ingenuity of expression, the command of language, the boldness of metaphor, which characterize Oriental swearing. There is something grotesquely horrible in the profusion of epithets and the manner in which maledictions are heaped on one's head, his eyes, and the various members of his body; on his parents and all his relatives and ancestors to the remotest generation; on his goods and possessions, his house, his horse, or his donkey, and in the obscenity that colors it all. The presence of women has little effect in checking it; the women themselves indulge in this little pastime in a manner to bring shame to the cheek of a modest woman. The Devil took the tremendous vehemence of Dante's "Inferno," mixed with it the terrific irony of Zoilus and Pasquino, then compounded with these certain hellish ingredients best known to himself, and lo! the result of the process is the profane swearing of the Levant.

Mr. and Mrs. Parsons, the only missionaries stationed at Nicomedia, gave me a very cordial welcome. The next day we crossed the head of the gulf and climbed fifteen hundred feet to the village of Baktchejík, an Armenian community among the mountains. It contains a good number of enrolled Protestants, but the whole place is to a great degree enlightened. There is a Protestant chapel on the brow of the acclivity, and, as we toiled up the steep, muddy road from the sea, on the calm air of evening we heard the musical sound of a church bell. It sounded like the church bells of New England. "That bell must have been cast in America!" was my exclamation; and sure enough it was. Five thousand miles away, some worthy people donated it to the villagers of Baktchejík, and now it rings among the mountains of Turkey, the harbinger of better things, the herald of peace.

We spent the night in a sort of backwoods style in a slight building constructed, like the native houses, of adobes, or sun-dried bricks, where Mr. Parsons spends the summer, as at that season the fever and ague renders Nicomedia unfit for a residence. Over a small pan of coals we boiled our tea and toasted our bread and our hands, the air, both inside and out of the house, not being of a nature to promote warmth, after which Mr. Parsons spent the evening in making pastoral visits.

The following morning we climbed still higher behind the village, to see the sun rise, and a magnificent prospect it was. All around us were mountains towering far above the point on which we stood, robed in snow and ice; and, as the sun rose higher and higher, peak after peak caught the spreading glory and fairly burned with splendor against the deep, cloudless azure of the sky. Below us the plain, the sea, and Nicomedia, gleaming in the distance, were half concealed with fleecy morning mist, that enhanced their loveliness like the white veil that scarcely hides the expressive eyes and delicate complexion of a Circassian beauty. We then walked back to the sea, and a light breeze wafted us across in little more than an hour.

The remainder of my visit was devoted to rambling around the environs of Nicomedia, and spying out its antiquities. In the reign of

Diocletian it ranked as the fourth city of the Roman Empire, both for size and sumptuousness. Diocletian made it his favorite residence until his retirement to Salona, and it was on the plain outside of the city that he finally abdicated his throne and went into seclusion. Nothing now remains to mark the former splendor of the town except its commanding situation, on the slope of four hills, with a lovely bay at its feet, half encircled with mountains five to six thousand feet high. The scenery reminds one of the Italian lakes. The Acropolis is yet surmounted by a ring of venerable towers, covered with luxuriant ivy, and fragments of the old wall remain far beyond the present limits of the city. There is still in excellent preservation the tomb of Valerius, an *actuarius* or quartermaster of the imperial guards, raised to his memory, as the inscription says, by his affectionate wife; and the sarcophagi rifled from the ancient cemetery, furnish troughs to the fountains of the whole neighborhood. The street pavement often contains marble slabs with inscriptions, and in the adobe walls of the houses or gardens, antique marbles are curiously incorporated. The tourist who is in search of beautiful scenery, enriched with interesting ruins and abounding in duck or other game, should visit the Gulf of Nicomedia in the last of the fall, or in winter and spring.

After my return to Constantinople, and during the last week in January, I learned that Mr. Parsons was to start on the following day from Nicomedia for a trip to Nicæa or Isník and the adjacent villages among the mountains. He takes this tour two or three times a year, and, as it extends through a rough district, and as he travels in a very simple way, it presented such attractions that I concluded to accompany him. But, on arriving at Nicomedia, and finding he had already a day's start of me, I decided to subtend the arc he was to go over in three days, and meet him at Koordbeléng. On Thursday afternoon my surrigee or guide brought the horses to the door; they were saddled with something that resembles the Mexican saddle, but the stirrups are set so far back as to make it agreeable for those who are accustomed to the European saddle to suspend them from the bow in front. In this way the Turkish saddle can be exceeded by no other in comfort for a long journey.

A trot of five hours and a half took us to Sabanjé, and we rode up to a coffee-house to pass the night. As it was the season of Ramazán, the annual fast a month long, during which Mohammedans neither eat, drink, nor smoke from sunrise to sunset, and carouse most of the night, the coffee-house was full of Turks smoking to a late hour.

> Let not a Soph'more think he smokes,
> Nor let a Freshman think he 's smoked,

until they have seen the solid blue tobacco-smoke in a coffee-house in the interior of Asia Minor.

These coffee-houses are built for the most part on one plan. A door at one end opens from the street into a large apartment with no other floor than the earth, beaten hard by the feet, and filthy to an indefinite degree. A divan, six or seven feet wide and several feet high, ranges along each side of the room, and is covered with a mat inhabited by larger or smaller swarms of vermin, according to the season. Winter is popularly supposed to have a benumbing effect on the aggressive disposition of fleas and "such small deer;" it *may* be the case. Opposite to the street door is the small fire-place where coffee is cooked, and next to this is the door into the stable. On entering, the guest makes his salaam and takes up his quarters on the divan, and the caffegee brings him a cup of hot coffee. Whether it is the effect of early education or not, the writer confesses to the opinion that neither the boasted French coffee nor any other boasted coffee is to be compared with the Turkish beverage. It is roasted as soon as possible before cooking, and is ground very fine, and even pounded in a mortar, if desired to be of extra quality. Enough for one individual is put into the water with the sugar in a metal pot holding about a gill. It is then allowed to boil or foam up three times; then taken off the fire and allowed to stand a minute; after which it is poured out and sipped as hot as convenient. Thus prepared, it is the most delicious of drinks for those who like it. For breakfast, it is sometimes cooked in the same way, but in a larger quantity, and with milk substituted instead of water.

After you have drunk your coffee, the caffegee brings a pan of coals and places it before you on the divan, if it is winter, and a narghilé, if so desired. Over these coals you warm yourself and cook your supper; then roll yourself up in your blanket and make the divan your couch, with your coat rolled up for a pillow. In the morning you have another cup of coffee from the caffegee, and, after paying for the coffee and the care of the horses a piaster or two — four to eight cents — you make your salaam, the caffegee wishes you Godspeed, you give your whip a crack, and start down the narrow street with a pack of dogs snapping at your heels. Such is the way the traveller fares in the interior of Asia Minor.

After supping and prescribing to a sick man, — in Turkey, all foreigners are presumed to have medical knowledge, — I rolled myself in my yorghân and snatched two hours of sleep. But a long shout awoke me; the Tartár or mail carrier had arrived from Constantinople, *en route* to Bagdad; and a few minutes later the clatter of hoofs and another shout were heard, and this time it was the Tartár from Bagdad who had arrived on his way to Constantinople. These Tartárs are picked men of fine appearance, dressed picturesquely and armed to the teeth. They travel day and night with one or two attendants, and with a train of four horses; they often carry money, and incur more or less risk of robbery. It had not been long before that the Tartár was murdered between Constantinople and Nicomedia. There was little sleep for the rest of the night, and we were off soon after dawn for Koordbeléng.

We passed through lovely scenery, Lake Sabanjé on our left and the mountains on our right; then through a fine forest of doddered oaks, on one of which we spied a noble pair of eagles, and toward noon we reached the Sakarius. This river is the second in size in Asia Minor, in width perhaps less than the Connecticut, but considerably longer. There is a Roman bridge in good preservation that once crossed the Sakarius, but now stands in a meadow several miles from the river, showing how its course has deflected in less than two thousand years. We rode down to the water through a magnificent gorge, and kept close to the banks for nearly four hours. Castellated rocks and jagged peaks towered on either hand, and far up in the blue flocks of eagles were seen sailing around the inaccessible cliffs. In past ages great armies have marched through this pass to the battle-fields of antiquity. Haroún al Rescheed, Bayazíd, and many other historic names, are associated with it. Remains of old fortifications still exist where the defile is the narrowest.

At the bridge of Geivéh, the place where Hadrian's favorite Antinous was born, we left the river and the post-road, and struck up into the heart of the mountains. The priests tell the people of Koordbeléng that they work out their salvation in climbing up the precipitous mountain sides to their village; and if works can save a man, the priests must be right.

Holding on to the horses' mane that we might not slip backwards, saddle and all, up we toiled. After getting up not less than three thousand feet, Koordbeléng hove in sight. Here we passed within a dozen yards of a large wolf, who was snuffing the mountain air, but before I could draw a bead on him he slunk away among the rocks. As we rode along the ridge to the town we had a sublime view down the gorges, snow-clad peaks on every hand, and hamlets on the cliffs, and were assailed by a north wind keen as a razor.

After a ride of nine hours we entered the place. Girls and boys, rosy, black-eyed, and picturesque, were clustered around the public fountain, filling their water-jars or sliding on the ice. For a backsheesh a boy piloted us to the room of the Protestant helper stationed there, and so steep, winding, and slippery were the streets that we had to lead our horses, both horse and rider slipping down in a confused mass every few steps. Hohannes, the helper, received me with the utmost cordiality, although an entire stranger, and I was soon installed on his divan, receiving the grateful heat of his mangâl, and brewing on the coals one of the best cups of tea ever concocted in Koordbeléng. In the evening some of the Armenians dropped in, and, what would appear rather singular to the tenderly-nurtured women of America who make a great bluster about woman's rights, the young women present sat in the cold corner, while the men were grouped around the coals, absorbing all the heat. At the risk of appearing ignorant of their customs, I could not resist the impulse to invite them to approach nearer to the fire; but it was of no use.

The next morning Mr. Parsons arrived, with the man who accompanies him in his trips, and surprised enough he was to find me in Koordbeléng. While he was engaged in conversing with the people, I devoted the day to climbing Bashilé Dagh, a peak of volcanic origin that towers many hundred feet above Koordbeléng. The snow on the summit was very deep, and the view surpassingly beautiful. On that elevated spot is the rude grave of some hero or magician whose burial-place legend has located there, and in summer it is a resort for pious pilgrims. The side of the mountain is diversified by several masses of rock resembling feudal castles, whose crannies are tenanted by eagles, and the scrub vegetation on the slopes teemed with hares and partridges.

On Sunday Mr. Parsons had over a hundred

to visit him and listen to his preaching, a larger audience than he has ever had before in that place. When he first visited it, eight years previously, twelve of the strongest men in the town, armed with clubs, entered the coffee-house where he intended to pass the night, and ordered him to quit the place instantly, on pain of something worse. It was in vain he showed them the safe-conduct from the Turkish government, ordering his free admission into Koord-beléng. There was nothing to be done but to leave. The Protestant helper who ventured to follow him was beaten from head to foot, and thrown out of the village for dead. He came to life again almost miraculously, and the government obliged the village to pay fifteen hundred piasters for damages and expenses. This touched them on a sore point, for they are exceedingly poor, and since then they have been more cautious in molesting Protestants. What is more, there are now two excellent men in the place, avowed Protestants, with their families; a number are on the point of forsaking their superstitions, and the greater part of the population is either friendly to the Protestant cause or indifferent to the old faith. Whatever facts may be urged to prove the inefficiency or wickedness of the Turkish government, it is but proper that it should have credit when deserving of it; and it is clear the missionary cause has made far more headway among the Eastern churches than it could have done if it had had to contend with governments as fanatical as the hierarchies of those Oriental churches that boast an apostolic succession, but have retained no attribute of Christianity except the name. There is very much less freedom of conscience in the Christian kingdoms of Russia, Greece, or Spain, than in Turkey. Whatever may be the reasons for this state of things, the fact remains, a fact to make one reflect. Should Turkey now come into the hands of Russia, the missionaries would have to desist from their labors in elevating the condition of the races of Turkey. The Christians under the Ottoman rule have been for many ages terribly oppressed; but Moslem subjects have also suffered greatly from misgovernment, which has been scarcely palliated by the circumstance that they are the dominant people and are maltreated by their co-religionists. In religious matters, with a few disabilities, such as being forbidden to have bells in their churches, the Christians have been left to their own devices. The Turks have been neither more nor less cruel to the Christians than other Eastern conquerors.

We breakfasted and dined at the house of one of the Protestants, of course seated cross-legged, eating out of the same dish placed on a tray on the floor, and waited on, as customary, by his wife and sister-in-law. He had three little children, named Martha, Mary, and Lazarus, and the whole family, as usual in the interior, ate, slept, and lived in one room, rolling up their beds during the day-time, and during the winter trying to keep warm with charcoal on a brazier or clay pan.

The poverty, the misery that one meets everywhere in the East is something beyond conception. If, leaving the ordinary routes of travel and avoiding the large towns, one visits only mountain villages, he sees nothing else but squalor and wretchedness, while even in the cities the signs of wealth and of foreign civilization are not too frequent. Every thing indicates the decline of an empire and the stagnation attendant on a state of society that has lagged behind the age. The average wages of a day laborer in Asia Minor are from three piasters to four and a half piasters a day; a piaster is just four cents; these wages do not include food, and out of them the peasant must support his family and pay enormous taxes. All who live within twenty or thirty miles of the post-roads which the government is trying to build, are obliged to work on them twelve days in the year and find their own provisions, or pay the equivalent in money; this is in addition to all their other taxes. A new house in a village is quite a phenomenon, and very few are ever built of any other materials than a framework filled up with sun-dried bricks, or wicker-work plastered with mud. A farm-house standing by itself at a distance from a town or village is rarely to be seen. The unsettled condition of society has always obliged the rural population to live in communities, often requiring them for this reason to spend half the working day in passing to and from their fields. Koordbeléng was once on the plain, but the frequent attacks of marauders induced the people to fix on its present almost inaccessible site. It is so situated on the brow of a precipitous slope, that it looks as if the whole village were about to slide off pell-mell into the gorge below.

On Monday morning, before sunrise, we were off for Nicæa. Our horses had been reshod, but they slipped down continually as we threaded the narrow lanes, while we clung to the house walls to keep ourselves in a perpendicular position. A number of friendly Armemans accompanied us out of the village, and from the brow of the mountain on which it is situated we saw the sun rise. Far below us lay the sleeping mist, and around us towered a circle of snowy peaks, sharply cut against the cloudless azure, and glorious with all the delicate variations of color, from a faint violet to purple, from purple to rose, and from rose to burnished gold that dazzled the vision. We walked down the mountain on the side opposite the one we had ascended in going to Koordbeléng, and galloped along the beautiful valley of the Sakarius until its second gorge came in view. Leaving this on our left, we ascended a ridge rising like a wall between this plain and the plain of Nicæa, and descended into the latter. The weather was superb; wild flowers were growing by the wayside, and we saw flax and wheat just coming up. It was curious to see the telegraph wires stretching over the country, the most wonderful result of modern science, while rude peasants were scratching the soil below with the primitive plow that was used in the days of Abraham. Towards evening, after ten hours in the saddle, we sighted the venerable towers of Nicæa.

After making arrangements to spend the

night at a coffee-shop, we sallied out for a moonlight inspection of the ruins of the place. A rich orange tint still lingered in the western sky, and the moon, now at the full, was so brilliant that I could see clearly enough to sketch by its light. I commend an evening stroll among the antiquities of Nicæa to one who likes a romantic walk by moonlight, among deserted ruins robed in mysterious shadows, and with the deep baying of shepherd dogs floating down on the breeze, or the long roar of surf on the shore, or the solemn cry of the muezzin and the melancholy hoot of owls perched upon crumbling battlements, thrilling the soul with a sort of weird sensation of awe and wonder.

The next morning Mr. Parsons sent on his helper to visit a neighboring village, directing him to meet us at Keremét in the evening. We then devoted the forenoon to a closer examination of the many interesting objects to be found in Nicæa. The present town or village does not occupy the twentieth part of the area inclosed by the old walls, and is of no importance except as the rendezvous of a weekly market or fair for the country around the Lake of Ascanius. The rest of the area is devoted to vegetable and mulberry plantations, weeds, reeds, marsh-land, ruins, storks, partridges, and snipe. The former city must have contained over fifty thousand inhabitants.

We went down to the lake side of the place and followed the walls around. Many of the towers, of which one hundred and eight belonging to the inner wall are still standing, are in excellent preservation and often profusely draped with ivy. These walls afford an example of the ancient systems of fortification such as cannot often be found elsewhere. Of the four city gates built by Hadrian and Claudius, three remain, opening on the Brusa, the Lefkeh, and the Constantinople roads. Each entrance is composed of two gates, the interior one being in each case of Turkish origin, while the exterior one is as invariably Roman, with fine archway and niches for statuary, and constructed throughout of splendid blocks of white marble. Many of the towers are composed of massive hewn stone, in some instances bearing evidence of having been rebuilt by the Turks of stones collected from Byzantine or Roman edifices. The Byzantine church of St. Sophia, where the famous council of the year of our Lord 325 probably held its sittings, is still standing in tolerable preservation, and is curious as presenting an example of the Basilican style of Byzantine architecture before it was modified by Anthemius and other architects of Justinian's time. A number of very quaint mosques and minarets also remain, relics of the Seljuks, the Turkish dynasty that ruled in Asia Minor at the period when the Crusaders besieged and captured Nicæa, and immediately preceded the reigning dynasty founded by Othmán. The vomitoria of the theatre still exist, four galleries converging to a common centre and constructed with almost Cyclopean massiveness.

Towards noon we walked up a hill in the rear of the town to take a bird's-eye view of the place, really a very fine prospect, — the cordon of ivied towers, and the lake bathing their feet and stretching thirty miles away, of a dark green and blue in the west wind that swept its surface, until it reached the snow-capped mountains in the distance. How often great armies have encamped on the plain below! How often the din of war has rung around those ancient walls, and mailed warriors have swarmed over the bristling battlements! During the last memorable siege over seven hundred thousand Crusaders beleaguered those fortifications that now stand dismantled and alone. The city was invested on the side of the water by galleys wafted from Constantinople to the Gulf of Gimlék, and then transported across the land and launched on the lake.

Soon after midday we remounted, and were off for Keremét. We rode most of the afternoon along the northern shore of the lake, through one of the most beautiful olive forests it has been my fortune to see. On our left lay the water, and its lulling and monotonous noise had a pleasing effect as hour after hour went by. On our right we passed the monument of Sestius, a pillar some sixty feet high standing alone on a plain. On a pedestal rests a shaft cut in the form of three triangular blocks or prisms, and a similar but smaller shaft surmounts this one, and tapers to a point. Further on we passed through a narrow, rocky defile noted as the haunt of brigands and the scene of many robberies. These fellows infest many of the roads of this region, and some daring robberies were committed a few days after we traversed the district. They are more or less in league with the villagers, and have their spies in the coffee-shops, who ascertain what travellers are likely to repay the risk of waylaying them. Missionaries are not usually of that class. Lefteri, one of the most notorious robbers of the Nicæan district, is called the

"Protestant brigand!" It may be for the reason that he condescends to read the New Testament. The following anecdote about him is true. One of his men was captured by the military by means of information obtained from a villager of Ovajík. Incensed at the loss of his henchman, Lefteri one evening decoyed the informer out of his house, collared and dragged him to a field out of the village, where he bound his captive. He next pulled out a pocket-Testament, read a chapter, and followed this with an extemporaneous prayer; after which he drew his sword and cut off the prisoner's right hand, bandaged the stump, and sent the man home. Mr. Parsons, on one of his trips, was met by a man bristling with arms, who demanded of him what was in his saddle-bags. "Books," was the reply. On this the man desired to see one, and sat down by the roadside and read awhile, apparently with deep interest. He then asked the price of the book, gave the money, and went off saying, "I came to get your money, and lo! you have, instead, taken some of mine!"

At nightfall we came to a hot mineral spring large enough to turn a mill-wheel, and steaming like a geyser. The roots of bushes growing near it were incrusted with a deposit of lime, and in many cases petrified. This was a sanitary resort in olden time; ruins are still seen under the water where the stream empties into the lake. Ruins, ruins, ruins! — the traveller meets them everywhere in these old countries. Scarce a garden-wall did we pass that did not contain marble fragments, often with sculptures or inscriptions; scarce a village cemetery of which the grave-stones were not pieces of ancient pillars; scarce a wayside fountain of which the trough was not an antique sarcophagus; scarce a field where the plow did not turn up marbles wrought by nations and generations that perished long ago.

We rode up the bed of a torrent, which is the principal street of Keremét, and passed from the pure air of the moonlight evening into the thick atmosphere of the coffee-house, two or three steps below ground, and crammed with steaming laborers smoking. As in many of these village coffee-shops, the windows were *glazed* with paper; stray sheets of the "Springfield Republican" have been actually impressed into this service. A sound sleep on the boards was refreshing, and we bathed our faces the next morning in a spring that bubbled out from the roots of an enormous plane-tree that stood before the coffee-house, and seemed to spread its giant arms over the whole village, like a venerable patriarch bestowing his benediction on the simple inhabitants. I might launch into raptures about the scene the previous evening when the icy range of Olympus, the nearer mountains and the Lake of Nice lay spread before us gloriously beautiful in the calm moonlight, but I spare the reader. Keremét is noted in this region for its oil, wine, and tobacco. Wine resembling Sauterne and pure as water from the brook, can be purchased there for a piaster the quart!

The following day we visited three villages, gradually getting up into the mountains again. At Ortakeuy, while Mr. Parsons was talking with the Armenians in the market-place, I went into the coffee-shop to smoke a narghilé, and found there a small circular sheet-iron stove, brought from Constantinople, modeled somewhat after imported Yankee stoves. In the midst of my pipe a rush of horses and voices was heard, and a brace of cut-throat looking Albanians came in, and began to bluster around and clear the divan of the idlers. They were shortly followed by a rather good-natured but lordly Turk, who was accompanied by a troop of swaggering Arnaouts, extremely picturesque, with their arms and kilts, but indescribably dirty. His majesty seated himself cross-legged on the divan, and was soon absorbed in an Oriental brown study. He proved to be a tax-gatherer going around to collect taxes, or rather to fleece the people. After a while he happened to observe me, and ordering me a cup of coffee, entered into conversation. My seven-shooter attracted his attention and collected all his troop around, who examined it with many exclamations of astonishment. Massive and rich as were their huge flint-lock pistols, their whole armory combined was scarce equal to a good revolver properly handled. The natives of Turkey are generally ignorant of the character of a revolver, and have a superstitious notion that it will shoot an indefinite number of times. It is safe to keep up the delusion. So delighted was the old fellow with our conference that he urged me to stay and dine with him in the evening off a glorious pilláf and a lamb that was to be roasted for the occasion; but our arrangements obliged us to go, and we rode off to Tchengilér, where we spent the night.

The ensuing morning, about sunrise, we were in the saddle, and instead of "flanking" the mountains by the road usually followed at this season, struck directly for the ridge, allowing the horses to pick their way up an ascent that was quite precipitous enough to please any one. We were soon among the clouds, which shut out a fine view of the Lake of Nice, the Gulf of Gimlék, the Marmora, and the Gulf of Nicomedia, which are to be seen from the highest point in clear weather. The descent was a ride long to be remembered, floundering through deep, soft, treacherous snow, and through pits of sticky clay up to the horses' bellies, or slipping from one almost perpendicular bank to another, or caught by some branch that threatened to tear the rider from his horse. Road or path there was none. After descending thousands of feet, we reached the village of Lelé Deré, where we rested half an hour. Mr. Parsons entered into conversation with the people, as usual. As we rode out of the town a savage dog flew at us, bit all our horses, and from a wall half sprung on my horse and made a grab for my shoulder. I put a ball through his body, and he became remarkably quiet. The shepherd dogs of the East are altogether a different breed from the vile curs of Constantinople. They are a noble race, faithful and sagacious in discharging their duties as guardians of the flocks and the villages, but they are the fiercest of their kind, and are often more than a match for the strongest wolf. It is almost touching to see how tenderly one of these rough animals will guard a flock of spring lambs, left entirely in his charge, keeping them from straying when the dams are away, and carefully refraining from biting or eating them, strong as must be the natural propensity to devour them.

By a detour we went over a plateau to the village of Sheksheh, of all the squalid places I have been in the most poverty-stricken; but, notwithstanding, Mr. Parsons sold a few Testaments there. The missionaries rarely give away books, because it is found that when the natives do not value them enough to make some sacrifices to purchase them at a small price, they abuse and destroy them if obtained for nothing.

We passed the night at Kurutch-Keuy, which we reached at sundown. The village school there is held in summer under the shade of a splendid walnut-tree. Our morning ablutions were performed at the public fountain, where the "rural maids" were laughing and chatting, filling their water-jars, or washing their clothes, while the flocks and herds were going by to pasture, enlivening the air with their bleating and lowing, and the tinkle of sheep-bells. The Armenians of the interior are generally a handsomer race than their sallow-faced brethren of the capital. The young men and the girls of these Armenian villages are often possessed of features strikingly expressive and beautiful.

At Kurutch-Keuy, as at most of the villages we visited, Mr. Parsons was greeted with a sincere and hearty welcome. He is well known in these parts, and his self-denying labors are slowly but surely bearing fruit. On every successive visit he observes increased enlightenment and growing interest in the truth which he proclaims.

A wild boar and jackals were seen in our ride the next day, and we passed a fine Roman bridge in excellent condition, built of brown stone, with parapets of marble slabs, well preserved. We brought up in the afternoon at Merdigóz. On the stilly air we could hear the shepherd's pipe, more mellow than the softest flute, more wild than the trill of the lark. From the mountains of Arcadia to the mountains of Circassia the same rude reed-pipe is the solace of the shepherd in his lone days and nights of watching with his flocks. Simple as is this instrument, the art of drawing music from it is confined almost entirely to the shepherds.

The Turks, smoking and playing cards in the coffee-shop, with loud vociferation and wrangling, kept us awake the greater part of the night. The one who lost was to pay for the coffee drunk, and after the playing was over, they spent nearly half an hour trying to beat down the caffegee five paras, or half a cent, and finding him inflexible on that point, they went off on another tack, and tried to prove that he should take off five paras from the score because, as they now claimed, they had only had fourteen cups instead of fifteen! Money is scarce and time abundant in Turkey.

Our next day's journey was sufficiently romantic, over a lofty ridge, and down into a deep gorge, where we forded a brawling stream twenty-four times; then over another ridge into another gorge, where we crossed another stream fourteen times. We passed through noble walnut and beech forests, and saw wild flowers, ferns, ivy, and luxuriant mosses growing by the side of the deep snow, — the signs of approaching spring. Many of the beech trunks were of the most grotesque, fantastic shapes imaginable, as if some genius like Gustave Doré had been revelling at will in these wild mountain passes, and contorted the trees to suit his own wayward fancy. After passing another noted haunt of brigands, in the afternoon we came out on the plain by the sea-side. Mr. Parsons and his attendant then turned up the mountain to Bagtchejik, where he was to preach the following Sabbath; I rode on three hours farther, and reached Nicomedia after being in the saddle eleven hours, and took a warm bath at once, a necessary precaution after sleeping in the filthy coffee-houses of Anatolia.

VII.

THE CROWN OF IONIA.

IT often happens that the dreams of our sleep make such an impression on the mind, and continue to appear so vividly before us in our waking hours, that they take us captive by a sense of reality, and an effort is required to shake off their influence; of more rare occurrence, but more powerful, is the effect produced when the reality seems like a dream. Once or twice at least in the life of most individuals, events or scenes pass before the vision so astonishing and bewildering, that one is at a loss to tell whether he is awake or asleep; instinctively he feels of his hands, his clothes, and other objects, to assure himself by tangible evidence, that he is wide awake and in his right mind, and even then is disposed to question the evidence of his senses.

Such was the peculiar mental state into which I was thrown when I went on deck soon after sunrise, and found our steamer anchored in the harbor of Smyrna; years had elapsed since I had last seen it. I had been forewarned that the place had changed, and, although aware how little that means when applied to a Turkish town, had prepared myself for the shock that one experiences when, on revisiting his old home, he sees the traces of "Time's effacing fingers" visible on many a cherished object. But I was unprepared for what met my view. Time had kindly drawn back the curtain which veiled the years that had fled, and I saw before me the quaint old town reclining as of old along the shore; the same red roofs and cypresses clustered on the hill-side; the same cafés jutted out over the water; apparently the same vessels were anchored here and there about the silent, solitary port; were not these the same men-of-war that from one year's end to another idled off the English quay, the roll of the drum in the gangway, and the musket shot on the forecastle at sunrise and sunset, almost the only sounds that broke the long summer stillness; and when I looked over the side of the steamer, the illusion was complete; there were the broad, sharp, decked surf-boats of Smyrna gathered around the ladder, waiting for pratique to be given us, — the most familiar sight I had seen since I had left the place for America; more curious still, the first boatman to catch my eye was the one we had always employed, distinguished for his kindness, honesty, and skill. Inclined to keep up the illusion, which made every object seem like part of an intangible dream, I stepped to the taffrail and hailed him as in former days:

"Eh, Papathôpoolé, tee kâmnetté?" "Halloo, Papathôpoolé, how do you do?"

Having been informed that I was expected, he recognized me, and characteristically replied, —

"Toolôyo sas éné, chelebee? caïky thêletté?" "Is that you, sir? do you wish a caïque?"

We started for the shore; the villainous conduct of the custom-house officer who intercepted us was so perfectly natural, that I could have offered him a year's backsheesh if my enthusiasm had been able to settle the question with my conscience and my purse. A piratical looking knave in Albanian costume, with a huge brace of horse-pistols and an enormous dagger in his belt, he was in a caïque rowed by a similar pair of jail birds. Midway between the steamer and the quay this boat bore down on caïques from the steamer, ostensibly to examine all baggage, and prevent smuggling. Tackling to our boat, as if to come on board to overhaul the contents of my trunk, the officer demanded a backsheesh in the tone of a brigand levying black mail.

"Here is my baggage; and here is the key; what more do you want, janúm?"

"What do I need of your trunk? give me a backsheesh?"

I flung the fellow a coin, pleased to escape the bother of unlocking the trunk. Picking it up, he turned it over in his dirty palm, and was about to raise his demand, when another boat going by with several passengers called off his attention, and he started in pursuit, bawling lustily for them to stop. In Constantinople there is a little more strictness in examining baggage, because the customs are mortgaged to Europeans; the officer comes aboard and has the trunk opened; but as the lid is raised, a backsheesh should be dexterously slipped under, so as to be the first object visible on looking in. This manœuvre at once results in the surprising discovery that the baggage contains nothing contraband, and the officer returns to his own caïque with a polite salaam.

As before observed, so exquisitely characteristic was this little episode, that it rather tended to keep up the enchantment that had woven itself around my senses. Many new residences have been built, chiefly around the

"Point," but still, when I sallied out after breakfast for a stroll down Frank Street, the Marino, and the bazaars, the alterations I found here and there were scarcely perceptible enough to disturb the waking dream which continued to haunt me during the remainder of my stay, and made Smyrna still appear what memory had pictured it, one of the most charming and unique residences in the Levant, and in the world.

Who has not eaten the figs and the raisins of Smyrna, the "Ornament of Asia," the "Crown of Ionia?" Situated at the head of a broad, beautiful bay, environed with perennial gardens, girt with a diadem of lovely villages, fragrant with the odorous airs that lade the serene Ægean skies, dowered with the wealth of historic associations, still dispensing fruits to the world with a liberal hand, watched by the old Roman citadel, the grim battlements of the Knights of St. John still reflected in the waters of her port, Smyrna, the city of the Moslem, the Greek, and the Frank, is a living poem, but a poem of Byron's, fervid with the romance, the passions, and the crimes of the East. He who has sojourned there for a fortnight, dreams of her in his subsequent travels, and he who has happily dwelt there for years, longs for her in other lands, and sighs that destiny separates him from the vineyards and olive groves, the villas and ruins, the Caravan Bridge and the bazaars, the delicious breezes and star-eyed maidens of Smyrna. With such kindness does she welcome the child of the West to her bosom, that no city in the Levant can boast so large a proportion of foreign residents. So considerable, in fact, is the Christian population, that the Turks call the place *Gheaoor Ismír*, — Infidel Smyrna.

There are antiquities in and around the city of sufficient interest, chief among them the walls and towers of the castle crowning the brow of Mt. Pagus, immediately in the rear of the Turkish quarter, which are well worth visiting. From the old ramparts a magnificent view is obtained over the city below, the gulf stretching far away encircled with mountains, and the gardens and villages, whose verdure gives life to the prospect. Near by are the remains of the ancient stadium, where Polycarp was burned, and where many other Christians steadfastly endured the onset of wild beasts and the horrors of the stake. But the real charms, the fascinations of Smyrna, are to be found not so much in what she possesses to remind us of the past, as in the softness of her climate, and the peculiar life led by its inhabitants, and this can only be thoroughly appreciated by those who devote more than the tourist's usual four or five hours to visiting this city.

In the days when the Janizaries were a sort of standing threat against the life of any Christian, and foreigners lived in Turkey almost as secluded as they did so recently in China or Japan, the English, French, or Italian merchants had their magazines and dwellings built on narrow, high-walled courts, extending from Frank Street to the Marino or Water Street, each end of the court being guarded by massive iron-studded gates, that are closed at nightfall; every court has also one or more porters who carry the merchant's goods by day, and mount guard for him at night. They are magnificent fellows, rarely under six feet in height, proportionably sturdy, with heavy beards, and as nearly the descendants of the stock of Othmân as any in Turkey. They come from Ushák and Aidín; the former is the place where the famous Turkey carpets are made. When a boy is born there, it is the wish of his relatives that "he may become a good Smyrna hamâl." On reaching manhood he goes thither to live until he has amassed sufficient to enable him to return and pass the remainder of his days under the patrimonial fig-tree. The weight these porters carry on their broad backs is something enormous.

The magazines on these courts are usually one story in height, and on part of the roof, which is flat, the house is built, the remainder of the roof serving as a sort of hanging garden on which to keep flowers, to promenade, or to sit at evening and watch the sun set over the sea, to smoke, take coffee, and chat. These terraces are also admirable positions for kite-flying, which is conducted in Smyrna on a scale unknown in most parts of the world. The kite season begins towards the last of February, and continues until May. A hundred kites may sometimes be counted at a time in the air, and what gives to the pursuit a singular interest is the circumstance that the Smyrniote manœuvres his kite as he would a boat or a horse, and kites may often be seen fighting in this way for hours. Great skill and practice are requisite in the construction and management of the kite for this airy warfare, which is not confined to boys, but is also engaged in by older persons, and thus forms a sport far more exciting than the insipid mode in which they follow this sport in America, unless we except "kite-flying" in Wall Street, which is said to be exciting for those who participate in it.

During the fig season some of the courts are the scene of a spectacle that is interesting to such as consider dried figs one of the indispensable luxuries of our Thanksgiving. Large quantities of the fresh fruit are brought into Smyrna on the backs of camels, which march solemnly through the narrow streets in long processions, to the monotonous beat of a bell fastened to the pack-saddle of the leading camel. In front of each string of camels trudges a meek, carmelite-looking little donkey, across whose back strides the camel-driver, with a huge turban on his head and an enormous sheep-skin cloak on his shoulders, beating the leathern sides of the imperturbable beast with his long legs in unison with the clang of the camel-bell. Thus the slow train moves into the court of the foreign merchant or shipper, and the camels, after much grumbling on their part, are made to kneel down and deposit their cargoes. Since the railroads to Aidín and Kasabá have been opened the "ships of the desert" have had some of the wind taken out of their sails, but it will be a long while yet before they are entirely superseded. For a time, indeed, the railroads stood no chance, so high were their rates for freight, but experience has taught the managers wisdom.

The figs, which have either green or purple skins and are pulpy and pear-shaped, when they are fresh, are steeped in a solution of salt and water and placed in heaps on mats laid on the pavement of the court. Around these mats women from the country collect, sitting on the ground barefoot, and working over the figs with their fingers, each fig being thus manipulated and prepared for packing. These women are accompanied by their children, who nurse while the mother is at work, or sport around, also barefoot and greatly in need of a good washing, and occasionally, while scuffling, they chase each other over the mats on which the figs are piled. It is a very amusing sight to those who do not intend to eat any of the figs.

After this kneading process, the figs are packed in drums, the smaller ones at the bottom, a layer of superior figs and a few olive leaves being laid at the top to take the eye of of the purchaser. Fruit in Smyrna does *not* "grow bigger downward in the box." A few drums are filled entirely with the best quality of figs for those who choose to pay for them. The drums are carried to the quay and taken out to the ships in lighters. The manner of getting them on board is unique. A plank is swung over the ship's side half way between the lighter and the gunwale, and a man is stationed on this plank. There are also two men in the lighter. One of them picks up a drum and tosses it to the other, and he throws it to the man on the plank, and he to a man at the bulwarks, who tosses it to a man standing at the hatchway, who drops it into the hands of a man in the hold, who pitches it the stevedore. The effect is very odd, as the process goes on hour after hour with the regularity of a piece of machinery. When a house is roofed in the East, the tiles are sent up to the roof in the same manner, men standing on the ladders and scaffolding to catch the tiles; and although the operation is done rapidly, I have never seen either a drum or a tile drop from the hands of the catcher.

For the most part, the Christian quarter of Smyrna, the largest portion of the city, is now laid out with some regularity. The streets are wider and better paved than formerly, and lighted with gas, and the houses are solidly constructed of stone, somewhat after the Italian style, usually comprising two lofty stories. The large central hall of the ground floor is chequered with blue and white marble, which is both cool and elegant in its effect. A pleasant Smyrniote custom it is at evening for the family to sit at the open door and chat with their neighbors. This easy familiarity, this gossipy neighborliness, may not be consistent with the highest kind of civilization, or, at any rate, with the reserve of our race, but it has its charms. On holidays, which are both numerous and carefully observed by the cessation of business, the doors and windows are "clustered with women" "all abroad to gaze," eating confectionery and richly attired. One may see on such a day many expressive and beautiful faces, particularly among the Greek women. The Caravan Bridge is the favorite resort of the Smyrniote in his hours of idlesse; on the banks of the Meles, a stream of classic reputation, lined with cypress groves, willows, and cafés, great is the consumption of coffee, rakee, sherbét, lemonade, orgeat, rahat-el-lo-koom, and tobacco.

During the summer Smyrna would be a very warm, uncomfortable residence were it not for the sea-breeze or inbât which rises every morning, and, after blowing freshly all day, subsides at sunset. The many beautiful villages at easy distance from the city also afford delightful retreats for nine months in the year. The railroad now approaches several of these and facilitates communication. Many of the houses in the villages are planned with a delightful adaptation to the climate. The dwelling is shaded with the dense foliage of the mulberry and the linden, and faces east and west, with an ample, vine-hung portico and garden on each of these sides. In the forenoon the family can occupy the west front, and in the afternoon they can retreat to the shade on the east side of the house. Some of the gardens have fountains diffusing coolness and the music of dashing waters through the emerald gloom, while the cicada in the heat of the day keeps up her steady hum, that seems to render it still more "the land of drowsy-head," and invites the siesta of midday.

Nothing can exceed the abundance of fruit — grapes, figs, apricots, melons, cherries, and pomegranates — which is to be found in these villages of Smyrna. For six months in the year, grapes of many excellent varieties can be purchased for one to two cents a pound. The peasantry live on little else but fruit, poor cheese, and coarse brown bread for the greater part of the year, as, indeed, is the case throughout the East. Another circumstance to delight the eye in spring is the profusion of wild flowers that carpet the fields before the grain has yet attained its growth. Miles and miles are crimson with wild poppies, or white with daisies as if covered with snow, interspersed with forget-me-nots, anemones, harebells, vetches, and numerous other brilliant plants. The arbute also gives additional life to a Smyrna landscape; not the arbutus of America, but a large shrub with very bright green foliage and round berries the size of a strawberry, of vivid crimson, and rather agreeable to the taste. The laurel, also, with its flowers resembling the blossom of the orange both in appearance and odor, diffuses its fragrance along the roadside when the almond-tree blooms, towards the last of February, and the oleander borders the banks of streams with its luxuriant clusters of delicate pink flowers.

One of the most delightful Fourth of July's within my recollection was spent at the village of Bournábashy, about four miles from Bournabát, where we were passing the summer. At an early hour we started, forming quite a cavalcade as we clattered in single file through the narrow, crooked lanes of Bournabát. Some of the graver members of the party were mounted on horseback, but most of our number were on donkey-back. In several instances a pair of panniers were slung on either side of a donkey, containing children too young to ride a saddle, whose curly heads just appeared above the edge of the basket. One lad, proud in the possession of an American flag, waved it aloft at the head of the procession; and the effect of the whole was increased by the donkey drivers, who ran alongside of the donkeys, holding the ladies and children on the saddles, yelling at the poor brutes and thwacking them lustily Sometimes a donkey more ambitious than the rest would try to pass the others, "braying loud and clear:" this movement would produce a general rush, followed by a jam in the narrow street, or the pell-mell gallop of the whole party around an abrupt corner in the most comical manner, but at the peril of bruising our heads against some projecting wall, or crushing our feet to a jelly. However, as we passed out of Bournabát into the open country, we subsided into a gentle trot, and rode merrily over the plain.

In passing through Narlé Keuy, a hamlet on the road, the same scene was reënacted, every man, woman, and child in the place turning out to catch a glimpse of a spectacle that made quite a ripple in the monotony of their lives. Some burly camel drivers, smoking under a plane-tree while their camels were drinking at the village well or stretching their long necks to crop the overhanging foliage, ejaculated, "Mashallah," "May the blessing of God be with you," and other pious exclamations.

An hour's ride brought us to Bournábashy. Winding through a narrow lane, we emerged into the large common around which were built the rude houses of the peasantry. Although these dwellings were poor enough, yet they looked rural and homelike, facing the green, each in an inclosure of its own, and half concealed by the mulberry foliage and trellised grape-vines through which peeped the red tiles of the roofs. At the lower end of the village arose several enormous plane-trees, towering to a great height and throwing the pleasant shade of their far-extending boughs over that part of the hamlet. A small army could encamp under the largest of these patriarchs of the plain. A brook rambled along the green, until under these trees it was arrested in its course by a sort of basin, where it formed a pool in which the women of the village were washing their clothes. Standing barefooted in the water that played crystalline around their ankles, they soaked the clothes and then beat them on the white, smooth slabs of the cistern, all the while laughing and gossipping in the most artless manner. It was one of the most delightfully rural scenes I have ever witnessed, vividly reminding the observer of Nausikaa washing at the stream ages ago. A little farther on the brook, escaping from the basin and rippling over its clear, sandy bed, wound through gardens where melons and grapes grew in abundance, and there, under the mulberry-trees, we came to a halt. Rugs were spread on the ground, and the provisions brought were taken out of the baskets and prepared for dinner, while the juvenile members of the party hung out the Red, White, and Blue from the highest branch overhead, explored the neighborhood, feasted on grapes in the vineyards, waded in the stream, and dove into the thickets.

Dinner presented a curious and tempting melange of American and Oriental viands and fruits, followed, according to the invariable custom of the East, by coffee furnished by the caffegee of Bournábashy, and winding up with speeches and patriotic songs enthusiastically rendered.

Towards evening we remounted, and reached home by moonlight, some of the children being found asleep in their baskets when the cavalcade arrived at Bournabát.

The foregoing may serve to convey an idea of the simplicity and out-of-door nature of Smyrniote life, which is more or less characteristic of all classes. In that genial climate the peasant reaps two crops in the season with little labor and poor implements; by more steady application and fewer holidays, he might have greater returns, but to what end? The government would seize his harvests, and he would be no happier; and so in many other employments. Therefore, on gala days the best suit is brought out, and all is forgotten in the enjoyment of the passing hour. How often on sunny days have I watched the boats sailing to Smyrna from the opposite shore of Menemé and Karseeyaka, scudding in before the cool inbât, and laden with water-melons and peasants. From afar, over the water, one could hear the beat of the rude drum they bore, a red clay jar whose mouth was sealed with leather painted green. Thus hour after hour they would glide along with music and song, galliard and free of thought and care. It may be said that this is a low sort of happiness for intellectual and immortal beings; very likely; and it may be urged in addition, that the ordinary life of the workingman of Turkey is attended with much hardship and oppression, which should elicit the sympathy of the philanthropist; but the distinctions between the different grades of happiness are exceedingly nice, involving a question of metaphysics: if we look simply at the relative happiness enjoyed by the people of America and the oppressed races of Turkey during their mortal lives, we are inclined to think the balance hardly in favor of the former, who have different, and possibly more elevated recreations, but also more anxiety, worry, and vexation of spirit.

This train of thought was particularly suggested as I heard the Smyrniotes congratulating themselves concerning the railroads, that after much effort and expenditure of capital, they have succeeded in laying to Kasabá, in one direction, and to Ephesus and Aidín in another; these two short roads, and the very brief one from the Danube to Kustendjee, are the only railroads in Turkey. By these railways a gradual improvement in the commerce and condition of the Smyrniotes will become perceptible in the course of time, but whether the sum of their pleasures will be proportionately greater, I felt inclined to doubt.

One of these railways runs through Paradise; this may sound a little startling, but, from the general disinclination of the race to travel in that direction, I do not imagine that the announcement will produce any sensation or increase the travel on the road. However, lest some of that class who patronize Hawthorne's Celestial Railroad, should betake themselves to Smyrna for the sake of securing a short cut to heaven, it may be proper to add that Paradise is a clump of verdure shading a few farms just beyond the old Roman Aqueduct, in the lovely valley of St. Ann, on the way to Boujáh and Sedy Keuy. The reader of Xenophon will recollect that he uses the word Paradise to represent a park. By following up this railroad, one reaches the site of Ephesus, now called Ayiá Soolook, where some interesting ruins have been unearthed by the English engineer who surveyed the road. Great was Diana of the Ephesians, but neither the chaste Diana, nor Alexander the coppersmith and his vociferous fellow-citizens, have availed to prevent the advent of the iconoclastic Briton, and the progress of the iron steed who marches round the globe, the herald of advancing civilization.

It is evident that by slow degrees the social and moral condition of the Smyrniotes cannot but be affected by these various agencies so contrary to the traditions and spirit of the

East. However, ages must elapse before any radical change can be wrought in the character of the people; their outward customs and mode of life may to a certain degree conform to modern and western habits, but even after divesting themselves of their present Oriental customs, the climate will always have a tendency to soften the angles which are so strongly developed in the people of northern Europe and America, and will impart more geniality to the tone of society than is usually found in those lands, while on the other hand the society of Smyrna would not be injured by the admixture of more Saxon integrity and order into its composition. The party for reform clearly have the question when the morals of the Smyrniotes are under consideration; these will be the last traits of the Smyrniote character to feel the salutary influences of modern and Christian civilization. It would be quite worth while for the Smyrniotes to travel more frequently on the road to PARADISE than they are inclined to do. But they have very bewitching means for stopping the mouth of the severest critic; the rose conserves of Smyrna turn the words of censure that fall from the lips of the moralist, into laudatory phrases. In the month of roses imagine baskets full of rose petals ranged along the streets for sale, and lading the air with perfume; such a sight may often be seen there. A pound of sugar to a pound of rose leaves; keep over the fire until cooked; then deposit in a gilt glass jar, and put under lock and key for safety from children; pass around on a silver salver when occasion requires, with a glass of cold water, served up by a piquant Teniote maid; such is the most approved recipe for preparing and disposing of this delicious confection.

The backlavâ of Smyrna is another delicacy that might soften the asperity of Timon of Athens; it is a pastry, diamond shaped, containing almonds and spices, and flavored with rose-water and honey; it melts on the tongue. During the holidays of Bairám, at Easter or New Year's, at a christening or a wedding, a large tapsee or circular pan of backlavâ is one of the indispensable delicacies of the season.

The katymerry is another pastry, prepared in Smyrna with peculiar excellence. Early in the morning men go about the streets crying "*katymerria*," which are eaten with the cup of Turkish coffee taken in bed, or immediately after rising. I have heard an enthusiastic

Smyrniote, who had been educated in America, and was conversant with the cuisine of various countries, say that "he who has not eaten katymerria knows not what is good." The consumption of this article is for the present limited, as the overseer of weights and measures has prescribed so low a price for the size that the bakers find it unprofitable to make it. The bakeries of Smryna, as throughout the East, afford much entertainment to the observer. The whole front side of the shop is open to the street summer and winter; the broad counter, on which bread and pastry are rolled out, partially overhangs the pavement; behind it is stationed the baker at work; before it, in the street, stands the customer purchasing loaves or eating katymerria ; the oven is just inside, behind the baker; he lays the bread on the red-hot floor by a long-handled shovel, which projects far into the narrow street as he suddenly jerks it out of the oven, at the risk of hitting some passer-by. All the baking of the city is done at these public ovens, including meat and bread for private families. The loaves are carried to the oven in long troughs borne on the shoulder. Sesamé oil enters largely into the pastry of Turkey; the flavor is rather agreeable, far more so than the taste of the olive oil which impairs the cookery of the East during Lent and Fast days. The tomato is also an ingredient of most of their dishes; for six or seven months it grows in great quantities, and the essence of the tomato is reserved for the rest of the year, by extracting the juice from the tomato, salting, and then keeping it in the sun until the water has evaporated. The multiform excellencies of the tomato are as yet unknown in America, where a wretched stew of half-heated tomatoes floating around raw fragments in a watery, tasteless fluid, is the usual mode of serving up this delicious vegetable.

While dilating on the varied social and culinary attractions of Smyrna, it is well to give also a glance at what may by some be considered inconveniences liable to detract from the charms of residence there. The heat, locusts, earthquakes, and brigands would perhaps disturb the equanimity of those who are not like the Smyrniotes, accustomed to such trifling matters. I have seen the locusts so numerous at noonday that they darkened the sun, and filled the air like flakes in a driving snow storm, as they rushed by with a sound like distant thunder. I was covered with them in walking through the streets of Bournabát; if they alighted on a field or an orchard, in five minutes not a leaf would be left, and the houses were overrun by them; the country was smoky with the fumes of sulphur and brush-wood that were burned to drive them off. Fortunately such visitations do not happen very often, although locusts in considerable numbers are seen every year.

As regards earthquakes, Smyrna has been partially destroyed by them several times; early in spring slight shocks are expected as a matter of course, but occasionally there is a more awful visitation of this terrible scourge. I have felt the earth trembling for two weeks with scarce any cessation, accompanied by severe shocks once or twice a day. Walls and chimneys were thrown down, the earth opened in the neighborhood, and half the city went out and lived in booths. Of all events that make man realize his insignificance, and the power of "the voice that rolls the stars along," is the earthquake, whose rude shaking awakes the slumberer from his dreams at midnight with a roar as of the grinding of mountains to powder, and a crashing as though creation was falling about his ears. It is still more fearful when one is lying awake on a still night, and hears in the distance a rumbling sound, preceded by the yelping of innumerable dogs and the clamorous cackling of fowls, that have been aroused by the ominous murmur; onward it comes; the casement of the window begins to shiver; scarce is there time to leap horror-stricken from the bed to the door before the house is quivering and shaking to and fro; a few seconds of agonizing suspense and the earthquake has gone and left the roof still secure overhead. By this time, perhaps half the populace are in the streets screaming, "Kyrié Eleïson," "Lord have mercy." In a few minutes there may be another shock, but most probably it is not repeated for weeks or months. In the last century the French consul at Smyrna was giving a grand dinner in honor of his sovereign's birthday. In the midst of the banquet the earth opened, and the house with all in it was swallowed up. But the Smyrniotes become accustomed to these things, and their motto is, "Sufficient unto the day is the evil thereof." Happy is he who is so constituted that he can divest himself of unpleasant recollections.

As for the brigands, they constitute a nuisance that may be abated in time; there is not a land in the Levant that is not infested by these pests of society, who will only totally disappear when the character of the government has become entirely transformed. As related on a previous page, the Franks of Smyrna have been accustomed to spend their summers in the suburban villages. Hares, partridges, and wild boars fell at the crack of their rifles on the mountains, and they lived as if lords of the soil, receiving from the peasantry the deference awarded to foreigners, particularly the English. But some years ago a change came o'er their dream of content. Brigands were rumored to have been seen in the vicinity; then news came that the Tartâr, or government mail carrier, had been waylaid and murdered on the road to Ephesus. The robberies became more frequent, and gradually approached the outskirts of the city. At length all Smyrna was thrown into an uproar by the intelligence that M. Van Lennep, the Dutch Vice-Consul, had been carried off to the mountains, subject to the payment of seventy-five thousand piasters. Sauntering one afternoon in his vineyard, a stone's throw from his villa at Seddy Keuy, gun in hand, and accompanied by his children, he was instantaneously surrounded by armed men, who seemed to spring out of the ground. The children were allowed to return home, while he was conducted into the wilds of Anatolia. The messenger who carried the news to the city, was the captive's gardener, and he was enjoined to bring the ransom within thirty-six hours, as he valued his own and his master's life. Pending the absence of the gardener, M. Van Lennep was hurried from one mountain to another, — his captors being constantly on the alert against the appearance of a troop of soldiery virtuous enough to attempt his rescue. He was treated with all civility, and found his entertainers armed with Belgian rifles, and provided with London spy-glasses, through which he was permitted to gaze from the peaks of the Two Brothers on his own residence in Smyrna, like Christian on the Delectable Mountains, viewing the Celestial city through the perspective glass of the shepherds. On the payment of the stipulated ransom he was promptly liberated; but the Sultan was fain to compound this affair with the Dutch government, by presenting the insulted official with a superb gold snuff-box, richly mounted with diamonds.

Yanny Katerdgee was the chieftain who opened the campaign with such startling exploits; short, thick-set, and muscular, he was well adapted for the perilous career he had chosen. Encouraged by his extraordinary success, he and his band followed it up by a long series of captures, outrages, and alarms. Dr.

Macraith, a prominent English physician, was swooped up on a summer's day while hunting. He found that sporting may prove a costly amusement. Two ghostly fathers, members of the Jesuit Mission, were taking an airing one afternoon, on the crumbling Roman ramparts of the Castle Hill, within hail of the city and the quarters of the garrison. They were doubtless engaged in pious converse, as they gazed on the picturesque town and the lovely bay, flecked with sails, which lay at their feet. But their holy meditations received a sudden interruption. Many a nightmare and fit of indigestion they have doubtless endured since then, when calling to mind the experience of that evening.

The villages of Boujâh and Seddy Keuy were almost forsaken by the Franks. At night the brigands came down and danced with the servant maids in the country-seats of the English gentlemen. The English chaplain and his family were almost the only foreign residents who dared to pass the summer in Boujâh; but his beautiful daughters practiced at target-shooting. The eldest, however, was nearly carried off, and the family suddenly returned to town.

Nor was this all. In his "King of the Mountains," M. About says of Athens, "It was dangerous to go out of the city; there was even some imprudence *in staying in it.*" This was also true of Smyrna. The robbers were known by sight to many there, and might occasionally be seen in the streets, disguised as gentlemen in European costume, sporting canes, spectacles, and jewelry, and purchasing articles necessary to their profession. At Easter and other festivities of the orthodox church, the rogues were among the most devout at St. Demêtry's shrine, in Frank Street. Rarely did these pious varlets allow their consciences to reproach them, like the conscience of the ancient outlaw, —

> "Ze on thynge greves me,
> And does my hert myche woe,
> That I may not so solem day
> To mas nor matyns goo."

But more. The wealthy residents of the city occasionally received notes couched somewhat as follows: "M—— will find it to his interest to deposit six thousand piasters in such a spot by Thursday week. Disregard of this little request might prove prejudicial to his health." Such drafts were repeatedly drawn on the coffers of the first citizens of Smyrna by these kings of the mountains.

It may be very properly asked, why the knaves were not captured or dispersed; and the only reply that can be given will appear ridiculous to our order-loving citizens. It is not a trifling matter to ferret out these foxes from their philosophic retreats among the defiles of Mt. Sipylus, especially when the peasantry are more or less in league with them, and give timely notice of the approach of the troops; and when the latter, also, act on a tacit understanding that if the robbers go one way, the soldiery shall vigorously follow up the scent in the opposite direction. The rough Arnauot guards hardly consider a few cents per diem a sufficient "war risk," not to mention the douceurs from the opposite party that accidentally reach their pockets.

But if it is so difficult to entrap the robbers themselves, why not at least weaken their power by apprehending their most notorious accomplices in Smyrna? "What would you have," responds their unhappy victim, shrugging his shoulders. "If I denounce well-known villains, I shall fall by the dagger or the bullet; I am not prepared to sacrifice myself for the public good, because, forsooth, the government is inefficient."

Such has for years been more or less the

state of things in and around Smyrna. Sometimes, as at present, the band of brigands is dispersed and driven off by a sudden spasm of energy on the part of the military, and a few ruffians are strung up as an example; but the country is always to a certain extent unsafe, and the more quiet is the aspect of affairs the more there is reason to suspect that it is but a suspicious lull before the outburst of another storm.

Perhaps we cannot better illustrate the facts we have given than to offer a brief sketch of the career of one of the more noted of the Smyrna brigands.

Yanny, or John, Katchêky, was a native of Seddy Keuy, and his father was game-keeper to M——. No urchin of the village was such a depredator of the vineyards, the orchards, and the dairies. When he was eighteen he hired himself out to a wealthy Turk of the village as gardener. His master had a daughter who was beautiful as the new moon; her eyes burned like the eyes of a gazelle of the desert, and her hair was black and glossy as the plume of the raven. The sacred amulets and bracelets of Mecca never encircled a rounder arm than Zeinéb's; and beneath this lovely exterior beat a heart whose emotions were fierce and impulsive. Yanny was also young and handsome. The jaunty fez, embroidered vest, well-fitting leggins, and red shoes which he wore on holidays set off his fine figure to such advantage that it was an easy matter for Zeinéb to return his ardent glances with interest. For a time the lovers remained unsuspected, but they knew that their secret must sooner or later be revealed, and woe be to them when her sire should find them out; for never for a moment could he, a zealous Mussulman, allow his daughter to permit the advances of an Infidel. Zeinéb's mother, with feminine tact, discovered what was going on, but unexpectedly approved of their attachment, being herself weary of her lord. The trio decided to make away with him, take the family jewels, and join the brigands, with whom Yanny was already on familiar terms. The plot worked admirably; a dose of poison was successfully administered, the treasures were secured, and the murderers sought the nearest robber haunt.

This suspicious spot was among the precipices of Mount Tactalee, where the scream of the eagle and the howl of the wolf and the jackal blend with the brawl of the torrent that raves over its flinty bed in the lonely gorges.

The shades of evening had fallen over the pass, and a group of the freebooters were assembled in their stronghold: by the faggot fire whose fitful glare played on their features and threw their figures into strong relief against the gloom of the cavern, they snatched their supper, smoked, counted over the spoils of the day, and planned new exploits. A sound broke on the stillness. Steps are heard along the side of the mountain, and then the challenge of the sentinel: —

"Who goes there?"

"Yanny Katchêky."

"You are welcome, Yanny! but hold — who are those with you?"

"Oh, they are friends, — my little bird and her mother."

"Good; advance."

As Yanny came up, the band issued forth to see the new comers. When the banditti discovered the women to be Turkish, murmurs of dissatisfaction were heard; the brigands of the East are good Christians and also men of few words, and the chief, fiercely confronting Yanny, thus sternly addressed him: —

"Are there no Christian damsels in Smyrna that you should marry this Moslem jade? Now, by your soul, slay her on the spot, or I will make short work of you! Here is a pistol; let us see your pluck!"

There was no room for hesitation or entreaty, and the youth had no inclination to risk his own life for the sake of his paramour. The stunning report of the discharge rang from cliff to cliff blending with the death-shriek of Zeinéb; and at the same instant that she fell the chieftain's blade pierced her mother's heart, and the two were thrown over the precipice.

"Bravo! you will yet make one of us," exclaimed the captain when he saw the aptness of his pupil in woman-slaying. The band returned to the cave as if nothing extraordinary had occurred. Such was Yanny's terrible initiation into his new profession. That night with his new companions he started to waylay the mail-carrier; and before long, so naturally did he take to the business, he was accounted one of the leaders of the troop. After many exploits and adventures he decided to retire on a hard-earned competency. The island of Samos was the retreat he selected, and what place is more suitable for the residence of a retired bandit? The wines are superb, the women are fair, and the climate is salubrious. Above all, he could there find congenial company; for your true Samian is a *palikâré*, which often means, an adventurer, a bully, who can swell around like a turkey-cock, when the coast is clear, rob his neighbor on the sly, shoot his brother on occasion, and keep out of danger when necessary. Arrived at this island, Yanny settled down into an exemplary member of society; "the Devil a monk would be." He took him a wife of the daughters of the land and devoted his leisure to smoking, drinking minto, and discussing politics and women under the village plane-trees.

But the restless life he had led little fitted him for the sweets of seclusion and domestic felicity, and ere long Yanny was again bounding among the crags of Ionia at the head of a villainous crew. Making his way back to his native village, he found favor with the companions of his youth whom shrewdness or fear prevented from openly declaring themselves as brigands, but who with others in neighboring villages became accomplices with the robbers, and afforded them material assistance in the prosecution of their plans. When night came on Yanny and his comrades would descend to the hamlets, make love to the peasant maids, and dance and carouse till morning. Some of the rogues were valets who had plundered and then ran away from their masters; others had rendered themselves obnoxious to government; and some, as in Yanny's case, had entangled themselves in an unfortunate amour. There were to be found among them a number who possessed a tolerable education. But after a while, when the government found that it would not do to allow gentlemen to be whisked about the mountains without leave, it exerted unusual effort for the extermination of the robbers. Some were shot, others imprisoned, and Yanny concluded to make a trip to Athens until the storm had blown over.

We next find him playing the character of carrocierri or hack-driver under the time-hallowed shade of the Acropolis. After a few months affairs settled down to their old state again, the guards slept all day undisturbed, and Smyrna was reported at the capital as restored to order and tranquility. When every thing was quiet the foxes ventured out of their holes, and Yanny resumed his former vocation. But he was not destined always to pursue his career unmolested.

It was a summer's day in Boujâh. The trailing clematis and the jessamine drooped in the hot wind from the parched plains of the interior; no sound was heard but the ceaseless buzz of the cicada, and the musical sound of waters emptied by water-wheels into the dry cisterns. The Zeybéks stationed in the village were idling at the Konâk or guard-house, some sleeping on mats, others playing backgammon or watching the game. The agâh was seated cross-legged on his divan, curling his enormous moustache, and bubbling away at his narghilé, in a brown study about nothing. Were it not for the snoring of the slumberers and an occasional "vy! vy!" from one of the half-witted spectators, they might have passed for a company of automatons.

Suddenly a small boy rushed in and screamed that a party of robbers were lurking around Sperâky's vineyard. The agâh's features immediately lit up with joy, for he was of a martial turn of mind, and found but rare occasion for the exercise of his talents.

"Mashallah! God is great!" cried he; "up, my lions; let us give the keopéks a taste of powder."

In the mean time Yanny, unsuspicious of danger, was lying in the shade of an old olive, his carbine resting against the trunk. His men were creeping under the vines, and luxuriating in the grapes that hung "wanton to be pressed." All at once he caught the glimpse of a strange face peering at him around the tree; in a twinkling he was on his feet, but his weapon was gone, and he was surrounded by foes. Nothing was left but to surrender.

"Look here," said he to the agâh, "let me go and I will pay you five thousand piasters. If you heed me not it can be of no possible advantage to you; your valor will pass unnoticed by your superiors and I shall soon be free in some other manner. But now, if you hearken to my proposal, you have a sure reward for your trouble."

"Silence, dog of a Christian!" rejoined the other with singular integrity for a Smyrniote Turk; "hold fast to thy money as long as thou canst, for, by the beard of the Prophet, thou shalt rue the day that my shadow darkened thy face. So Allah help me, I'll see thy carcass hang from sunrise to sunset, for yonder raven to whet his beak on thy bones. Here," turning to his men, "bind the villain fast, for such quarry falls not in our hands every day."

It is hardly necessary to state that the rest of the brigands did not tarry to learn the fate of their leader, but evacuated those perilous grounds with surprising rapidity.

A few days after this event the agâh was

picking his way among the mountains, when a voice hailed him that sounded as if it came from the clouds. On looking up, he discovered his late prize balancing himself on a projecting rock.

"Good morning to you, my worthy friend," Yanny tauntingly exclaimed; "I am happy to thank you in person for the little journey you gave me the other day to the city. You see my head is still on my shoulders. Fine jailers are these countrymen of yours. I offered you five thousand piasters for my liberty, but you refused, and I gave my guard two thousand, and am again free to rove at my will."

"Ha!" cried the Turk, "so that's you, is it? I'll not risk my life again to catch such rogues; it proves unprofitable."

Some months later Yanny's career came to a termination well befitting the turbulent life he had led; the Arnauot guards again surprised him, and he fell by what was very likely a stray shot.

VIII.

FIOR DI LEVANTE.

IT was early in June that a needed change of air induced us to leave Smyrna and spend two months in the island of Scio, noted for the loveliness which gained for it the name of Fior di Levante, and for the horrors it sustained during the Greek revolution. An acquaintance on the island was requested by letter to procure a house for us, and the furniture we were obliged to carry was sent on in a Greek coaster hired for the purpose. By the politeness of the Turkish authorities we were permitted to take a deck passage on board of a Turkish government screw-boat of about fifty tons, which was transporting a company of soldiers to Samos.

We embarked soon after sunrise and glided quietly down the beautiful bay of Smyrna expecting to reach Scio by sunset; but by noon the wind, instead of veering around to the customary western inbât or sea-breeze, freshened from the north, until it blew half a gale. In expectation of the increase of the wind the topmasts were sent down, the yards were housed, and every thing was made snug. The soldiers lay around the deck or hung over the bulwarks in every stage of sea-sickness, and as we approached the mouth of the Gulf and Cape Kará Burnû the storm grew apace; the heavens frowned with blackness, the gulls were blown through the whistling rigging, the sea made a clean breach over the crazy little iron steamer, and what terrific waves are those short, quick, savage surges of the Egean! The wind blew down the Straits of Mytilene a hurricane, and directly in our teeth. After trying several hours to weather Cape Kará Burnû in vain, it was thought best to put back into Phôkis for the night.

As the steamer shot through the narrow entrance of the harbor, which was barely visible through the fast gathering gloom of night, she glided from a turbulent sea into a smooth basin, sheltered by surrounding hills. Here we found two large steamers of the Austrian Lloyds and the Messageries Imperialles, which had also run in to ride out the gale.

On coming to anchor, some of our party went ashore to find something to eat. Not a soul was abroad, and the few lights in the town shone with an unearthly glare through the mist. But we succeeded in picking our way to the coffee-shop, which was dim as we entered, except in the centre, where a pan of coals threw a partial light over the grotesque features of a group of sailors seated on stools or lying on battered mats around the fire, enveloped by a blue halo of tobacco smoke, and half dozing, half listening to the thrumming of a rude guitar. In one corner of the room lay several casks and skins of wine and rakee; in the opposite corner a small fire-place was built into the wall for the purpose of cooking coffee, and two or three carbines rested against the side of the house. Nets ingeniously cut from paper hung from the rafters, suspending Easter eggs; these were intersected by strips of paper scalloped and otherwise ornamentally fashioned of various gaudy colors, but now changed to a uniform dirty amber, and waving in the chilly gusts that made their way through the broken tiles of the roof. Such were all the attempts at decoration the public house of Phôkis could boast of, that celebrated Phokæa of old, whose name was famous among the cities of antiquity. Her mariners were the first, according to Herodotus, who made long voyages: they piloted fifty-oared galleys to the shores of the mysterious and unknown Atlantic, and it was they who founded Massilia, the Marseilles of our day.

After considerable chaffering with the tapster, a little goat's milk, a few eggs, and some coarse sour bread was all that we could procure besides coffee. With these supplies our foragers returned on board, and with the fragments of cold chicken remaining from dinner we managed to eke out a meal that was well seasoned with Spartan sauce. It is due to the Turkish captain and the other officers belonging to the vessel and the military company, to say that they treated our party with great courtesy, and when they found that the weather rendered a deck passage so disagreeable as well as hazardous to some of our number, they of their own accord vacated one of the two small apartments that composed the cabin, and crowded themselves into the other. The Turks doubtless have their faults, but many of the elements of noble breeding are to be found in the national character.

When we rose on the following morning the clouds were breaking up, but the wind was still strong, and we lay snug till the next day, killing time by strolling over the dirty little town. Idle women stared at us through lattice and gate, noisy urchins dogged our steps hooting after us, and pestilent curs snarled at our heels. In the outskirts we came across some pretty rural nooks, particularly a fountain shaded by poplars; a shepherd boy was sleeping under the whispering trees, while his flock nibbled the herbage and enlivened the impressive stillness of noonday with the tinkle of bells.

At cock-crow on the morning of the third day we put to sea. A dense bank of clouds, the last vestige of the gale, could be seen low down in the offing, its upper edge illumined by the approaching sun; a purple haze softened the deep blue of the sky, and the waters of the little port, now tranquil as a mirror, reflected the picturesque town, the grassy hills which environ it, the old fortifications crumbling on the shore, and the coasters riding idly at their moorings, while the morning star cast a quivering streak of silver across the harbor. As we looked back from the mouth of the port we saw the sun bursting above the hills, and heard the melodious voice of the muezzin wafted on the stillness of morn.

After a charming day on a sea surrounded by enchanted isles and gleaming with lateen sails, we anchored in Port Kastro early in the afternoon, and immediately went ashore. Through the narrow lanes of the massively built city we threaded our way to the town house of Mr. P——, the friend whom we had requested to find us lodgings. His aunt, who lived in the house, received us cordially, and a maid, according to the custom of the land, served us to water and preserves. Soon after we heard the clatter of hoofs in the paved quadrangular court below, and on descending found mules ready to convey us to the house hired for us in the midst of the Kampo, a plain stretching to the south of the town, between the eastern slope of the mountains and the sea, studded with villas. Mr. P—— mounted his donkey, a sleek, genteel-looking animal from Cyprus, and assumed the van, followed by the mules in single file, clattering slowly through the narrow streets, massive stone dwellings rising on either hand. We finally reached the open country, and, riding along at a gentle trot, proceeded to enjoy the beautiful prospects that continually greeted our eyes. Now we rode beside some stately gate-way, whose brow was engraved with the armorial bearings of a family that has gone to decay, while, through the half-open portal we could see the ruined villa which it guarded rising in melancholy grandeur. Again we filed by some little chapel embowered among flowering acacias and lindens, with the taper dimly burning within before the Virgin's shrine; or, as we halted by some Saracenic fountain to allow the mules to drink, we beheld luxuriant orange groves, with the fruit hanging on the boughs, "like golden lamps in a green night," and through vistas between the foliage caught glimpses of the blue sea beyond, and heard the songs of the laborers borne to our ears from afar.

In the course of our ride we passed by the country residence of the former Latin Bishops of Scio, which was erected during the rule of the Justiniani over the island. It is now stripped of the ornaments that once adorned it, yet it is lordly, even in its ruins; although roofless and with the sunlight and the rain streaming into its deserted halls, it speaks more for the glory of its founders than folios of musty vellum.

Soon we turned away from the road winding among the gardens, and cantered by the sea-side, the "many-voiced sea" of Scio's bard. We passed the vestiges of the entrenchments thrown up by the Samians who besieged the Turkish garrison in the citadel during the Greek revolution, and saw the peasants reaping their crops almost at the water's edge. After a delightful ride of an hour we reëntered the former road, and reached our "own hired house," situated beside the bed of a torrent that is dry except during the rainy season; as it is the main thoroughfare for the houses of the Kampo, stepping-stones neatly hewn and several feet high are fixed in the earth where the banks are too narrow to admit the passage of pedestrians when the water is deep in winter.

We alighted at the foot of a broad flight of stairs. Although built throughout of solid hewn stone with roomy apartments, the mansion was not so stately in its external appearance as many of the villas of the Kampo; but it had recently been put in a complete state of repair, and afforded comfortable accommodations, to say nothing of the orange plantation in which it was situated, and the magnificent prospect it commanded from the portico and the terrace on the flat roof. The ground floor was occupied by the overseer and his wife. A porter's lodge surmounted the entrance gate, communicating with the main building by a gallery running along the lofty garden wall, and amply atoning by its picturesque air for what was wanting in the appearance of the main building. For this establishment, exclusive of the plantation, we paid the enormous rent of one hundred piasters, or four dollars and a half a month. If all expenses in Scio were as moderate as rental, living there would be a trifling matter.

We found that our furniture had preceded us, and before long we were agreeably settled. In those warm climates a thousand things can be dispensed with which in America are deemed necessary to happiness and domestic comfort. Given a large house of solid stone, with broad stone floors and high ceilings, and plenty of cold running water to pour over the floors or to lull the senses at mid-day with its musical monotone; also bread, cheese, coffee, grapes, oranges, tobacco and conserves quantum sufficit; also a simple but ample divan to lounge upon by day and sleep upon by night; also a sleek mule whereon to take a constitutional on the sands after breakfast, and one is provided with very nearly all that is essential to comfort in Scio or almost anywhere else in the Levant for three fourths of the year. Many of the Sciotes, especially the peasantry, live in a much more primitive manner. The wealthier class have inherited from their ancestors superb villas of hewn stone, built after a mode combining the characteristics of the Italian and Saracenic styles in a very charming way, thus illustrating the successive rule of the Genoese and the Mohammedan over the island. A few Franks or descendants of the Latins and a few Turks reside in distinct localities, but for the most part the Sciotes are of the Greek Church, very bigoted and as a natural consequence generally illiterate, although before the revolution Scio rather took the lead among the Greeks in the matter of education, and Koray, the Sciote scholar, was one of the most learned and liberal-minded men of his age. It may surprise some to hear that in their features and many of their national traits the Sciotes do not altogether resemble other Greeks. Many of them have a Jewish cast of countenance, and it is by no means rare to hear them spoken of by other Greeks as a sort of mixed race, containing very little Greek blood. But nevertheless, they are more Greek than any thing else, and we see little reason to doubt that they are descendants of the Hellenes of antiquity, with some blending of Latin, Tartar, and Semitic blood. The peasantry are more Hellenic than the higher classes; they have a Greek dialect of their own, which they have doubtless spoken with little variation for the last twenty-five hundred years. It is an interestering fact that the little peasant village of Volissó, on the western side of the island, has existed with that name for thirty centuries or more. There, according to the ancients, Homer, the founder of classic literature, composed his "Batrachomyomachia"; and there, many centuries later, Koray, the great philologist of modern Greece, in his commentaries on the Iliad, gave a local habitation to his inimitable parish priest "Papa Trécchas," one of the pleasantest of satires on the illiterate clergy of the Greek Church. Is it not a phenomenon in history that an obscure village like Volissó should exist scores of centuries, outliving mighty cities and powerful empires, and presenting to us a self-perpetuating monument to the fame of the Great Minstrel? Let those who pretend that Homer never lived go to Volissó and repent of their sin! Some men waste their lives in trying to prove the Bible to be a myth,—the work of mere mortal, finite minds; it is a similar uneasy, cross-grained sort of disposition that inclines a man to devote himself to proving the non-existence of Homer or of Shakespeare. The arguments adduced certainly serve to show sometimes the ingenuity of the writer, and how much he might have done if he had taken up the right side, but in each case, granting all the difficulties that may be urged against either the divine authorship, or the identity of these poets, it requires far more faith to disbelieve than to believe the popular and accepted opinions on these subjects.

Soon after arriving in Scio we mounted our mules and rode over to the country residence of our friend Mr. P——, situated on the Kampo a few miles from our house. On dismounting at the gate, a groom led away the mules, and we were conducted up one of the magnificent stairways which so often in Scio remind one of Genoa the superb. The balustrade was of wrought stone, the steps were of marble, and the spacious portico to which they led was chequered by the same material. From thence we passed into a stately hall; a divan extended across the upper end, and the sunbeams stole here and there through the lindens that overhung the windows. As we entered into the apartment an elderly lady arose from the cushion on which she was reclining, and advanced to meet us; it was the mother of our friend.

Being absent from the island at the period

of the massacre, she had escaped its horrors, and returned when the disturbances had subsided, to find her husband murdered and her children lost. One son, however, who was at the time in a mercantile house in Trieste, still survived. Gradually they succeeded in partially restoring their shattered fortunes, and they found that their noble mansion had suffered but little from the vandalism of the Turkish hordes. After a number of years she heard that her youngest son was still alive; he was studying in the United States under the patronage of an American gentleman by whom he had been ransomed, and she soon had the inexpressible pleasure of clasping him to her arms. He it was who had so agreeably welcomed us to Scio.

She was arrayed in the pleasing costume of the Sciote females; her hair was slightly silvered by age, but her coal-black eyes still burned with their natural fire undimmed, and she repeated the tragedy of her life in the musical Hellenic tongue with a grace and dignity that reminded the listener of some peerless Helen, or imperial Zenobia, whose wondrous beauty and singular fortunes riveted the attention of antiquity.

After resting ourselves, the customary refreshments of water and conserves were passed around. We then adjourned to the portico, lingering there some time to revel in the magnificent panorama extended before us. In the distance rose the mountains of Asia Minor, of a soft violet hue; nearer spread the deep blue expanse of the Egean, lit with white sails; at our left a rugged chain of mountains rose grandly above the plain; and directly at our feet the Kampo rolled away to the sea, clad in the variegated verdure of the olive, the cypress, the orange, the lentisk, the linden, the mulberry, the pistachio, and the vine, with half-deserted pyrgoes or chateaus towering here and there above the groves. On the drowsy air came the sullen roar of surf on the beach miles away, and from all sides could be heard the monotone of the manganoes or water-wheels, as in every garden the patient mules, hour after hour, drew water from the wells for irrigating the soil; and occasionally a languid gust brought to us the scent of the orange-blossoms or the mild musk of the jessamine's silvery stars.

Oh the beauty and the glory of those landscapes of Scio! oh the softness of its clime, never too warm nor too cool! When did we tire of the loveliness that surrounded us?

when did the time pass wearily? Never! Our stay there was like a long dream of delight, an unbroken reverie, in a land where we fed on the lotus and drank the waters of Lethe; never before, never since, have I passed two months of such unalloyed happiness as the days that glided so quietly away on Scio's isle. In the morning we roved among orange-groves or galloped by the sea-side; we had our siesta at noonday, bathed in the sea at sunset, then watched the moon looming above the Teian shore where Anacreon dwelt and sang of old, and then lay "down to pleasant dreams."

Often in our morning rides we met the peasant maids in picturesque costume spinning as they rode or walked, with the shuttle under their left arm, and holding the thread and spindle in the right hand exactly as described by Homer in the following passage: —

> . . . . "As the running thread
> The spindle follows, and displays the charms
> Of the fair spinster's breast, and moving arms."
>
> *Iliad*, xxiii.

Not unfrequently we saw a woman mounted on a mule, singing lullaby to an infant at the breast, while another child sat behind her on the long, wide saddle, — still another curly-headed urchin clinging to the crupper, while the rude tinkle of the mule-bell chimed with the sportive voices of the children and the crooning song of the mother.

Mules are almost exclusively used as beasts of burden in Scio, and riding is very generally adopted. "If wishes were horses, then beggars might ride," is an old proverb which is literally interpreted in this curious island, for the beggars there came to our gate on mule-back, and found it difficult to understand that we hardly considered such a luxury as evincing extreme poverty.

In one of our rides we visited the house formerly occupied by the Rev. Mr. Hueston, missionary of the American Board many years before, when sojourning for a short season at the island for Mrs. Hueston's health. The house was uninhabited when we visited it, and was in a ruinous condition, but it was interesting to us as the temporary residence of the beautiful character to whose loveliness the traveller Stephens paid such a noble tribute in his travels. Mrs. Hueston is still remembered by the Sciotes as the good American lady. We were amused to find in this remote locality traces of American thrift. When Mr. Hueston occupied this dilapidated mansion he seems to have been annoyed by the air creeping through the cracks and crannies, which he accordingly plastered over with paper, and what was our surprise at discovering in this way dingy, antique sheets of the "Missionary Herald!"

Some days later we rode up to the monastery of St. Minas, which stands on the brow of a hill overlooking the Kampo. Into this convent three thousand Sciotes were decoyed by the proclamation of an amnesty during the revolution, and when the inclosure was crowded with the poor unsuspecting and unarmed victims, the Turks fell upon them and put them to the sword. We were cordially welcomed by the old monks who haunted the ancient cloisters like shadows of other days. They brought forth from their stores coffee and wine for their visitors, for it was not often that they looked on the face of a foreigner; and one old patriarch, an hundred and twenty years of age, related the various events of his long career. He described how, when a youth, in 1771, he had witnessed the destruction of the Turkish fleet on the opposite coast at Tchesmé by the Russians under Admiral Greig: he spoke of the American revolution and of the faint rumors of the great-heartedness of Washington which were wafted across the wide ocean to the little island of Scio, and how his bosom had kindled at the tale, and then, descending to the present century, he described with weeping eyes and quivering tongue how his native isle had been desolated by the torch and the sword, and how in that very monastery over three thousand of his poor countrymen were slaughtered without mercy. "There!" said the ancient in tones tremulous with grief and indignation, "there and there are the stains of their blood to this day!" and he pointed his shrivelled finger to the dreadful witnesses of that awful period still staining the marble floor of the chapel.

The father of Yoryé our gardener or overseer, was one of the few survivors of that massacre, and he described it to us in language simple but very pathetic, on a morning when we rode over to his tower in a leafy glen. His parents were butchered almost before his eyes. "How I escaped," he said, "I know not; the Holy Virgin watched over me; I leaped over the wall and fled. My father and mother I never saw again. May God have mercy on their souls! For days and weeks I roamed on the mountains alone; and I could see the vultures and kites hovering in dense flocks over the monastery — they were picking the bones of my friends!"

After burrowing thus in the clefts of the rocks he succeeded in escaping from the island in a Samian coaster with a fugitive maiden whose relatives had also been slain, and whom he married in Samos. From thence he wandered to Missolonghi, where he endured the horrors of its second siege, living on rats and old leather, fighting hand-to-hand with the Turks over the earthworks, and finally cutting his way out with the garrison through the enemy's lines, on a stormy night. He returned to Scio when matters became more quiet, sought out his father's house, repaired it, and had lived there ever since.

There is scarce a family in Scio that has not some such tale to tell of its fortunes in that massacre. Women are doubtless still living in the harēms of Cairo and Constantinople who were then sold into slavery, while their families have returned to occupy the ruins of their former homes and to live in ignorance whether their lost sisters are living or dead. Such is life here; in this Paradise we are constantly reminded of "man's inhumanity to man."

Scio at the breaking out of the revolution was the most flourishing island of the Egean. Port Kastro, the chief town, was opulent, and maintained a large commerce. The University of Scio was patronized by students flocking hither from all parts of the archipelago. The inhabitants were happy and contented, and were rather disposed to hold aloof from hostilities when the war commenced. As the island was an appanage of the Sultana Validé or queen mother, it might have weathered the storm if a band of restless Samians had not landed in Scio in spite of the wishes of the islanders, and laid siege to the Turkish garrison in the citadel. This exasperated the Turkish government to such a degree that they sent a large fleet against Scio and let loose 30,000 fanatical Turks to desolate this beautiful spot. Of course the Samians fled at once like dastards, leaving the unarmed Sciotes to destruction. In six weeks, out of a population of 100,000 nearly 70,000 had been slain or carried into slavery, while most of those remaining escaped to other islands, and Scio was virtually depopulated.

The island, however, has to a considerable degree recovered its former loveliness, and, with the exception of the ruins scattered here and there, the traces of its devastation are rapidly disappearing. The people, although much less numerous and wealthy than before the revolution, are generally contented, and are probably as mildly ruled as any under the Ottoman sway. They are, if possible, more devoted to the superstitions of their corrupt church than ever, and their saints' days and religious fairs and pilgrimages are observed with great care. Viewed æsthetically, with the eye of an artist, these religious fêtes afford much that is picturesque and entertaining. The groups of peasantry in their gay holiday attire, the booths fancifully decked with flowers and tempting with confectionery, the dances and the songs, — all present glimpses of the sunny side of the national character. If such occasions are too frequent in the East, it certainly is not the case among the more sober, phlegmatic, methodic Americans; and it may well be questioned whether a few more innocent holidays might not render our people more gracious in their manners, more contented and cheerful in their lives.

The Eve of St. John occurred during our visit in Scio, and in anticipation of the event the Sciotes spent the preceding afternoon in making preparations for celebrating the occasion with all the ceremonies and rejoicings established by custom; and our gardener and his wife, assisted by a party of their relations, collected a huge pile of brushwood in the dry bed of the torrent before our gate, against the arrival of evening.

In Scio the Roman Catholics, being under Latin protection, have long enjoyed the privilege of hanging bells on their churches, while those of the Greek faith, as in most parts of the Turkish dominions, have, in consequence of Mussulman prejudice against bells, been reduced to the necessity of using sounding-boards called sémandroes, on which they beat with mallets a sort of tattoo, when they summon the "orthodox" to their devotions. In Trebizond, in Nicomedia, in Brusa, in Scio, I have often heard this peculiar summons hammering away on holidays. Within a few years the native Christians have been permitted to use bells, but their poverty generally prevents them from availing themselves of the privilege.

On the evening in question, as the hour for vespers approached, the semandroes were unusually lively over the whole Kampo, resounding from the numerous little chapels situated in private gardens or by the wayside. Now the sounds died away to the distant valleys, now they swelled again on the sunset air, a numerous chorus of mallets keeping time to the prolonged tune; the effect was very peculiar and rather pleasing.

Some of our party attended vespers in a neighboring chapel. The little building was crowded, and many were standing without, bowing and crossing themselves, as the priest came to the door, swinging the censer among them and bestowing his pastoral benedictions. All we could do was to remain outside, snatching glimpses through the doorway of gilded pictures and flickering tapers scarce visible in the smoky air of the interior, while a confused hum was heard from the worshippers, blending with the chanting of the Litany. Having satisfied our curiosity, we prepared to leave, when a deacon, singling us out from the crowd, politely offered us some bread of wonderful whiteness, rich with the blessing of the bishop, to eat of which is considered a privilege. One of our number whimsically refused to partake, alleging by way of apology that he was not hungry; and he only complied after considerable urging; but the bystanders had heard his excuse, and great was the mirth it occasioned; we did not soon hear the last of it. The intelligence that a Frank gentleman had refused holy bread on the plea of want of appetite was disseminated over the island ere twenty-four hours had elapsed, as a bit of information too good to be lost.

With the arrival of twilight bonfires were lit before almost every gate, and the reflections from the various flames streamed up here and there through the foliage and up the sky like columns of light. Occasionally a rocket might be seen soaring in the distance toward the zenith, breaking and scattering a shower of stars over the groves; and the jocund sounds of merriment and festivity floated on the peaceful air of evening. It was a memorable scene.

In the meantime our gardener lighted the heap of brushwood before our gate. As the ruddy flames leaped upwards, illumining the graceful foliage of the china-trees which overhung the porter's lodge, the children and young maidens and youths who had assembled there, commenced an animated song, dancing around the fire, while a buxom damsel beat time on the tambourine; then the gardener and our servant Takvore fired pistols in the air, adding *éclat* to the spectacle.

But the feather-footed hours glided swiftly away, as is their wont when the soul is most free from care. Gradually the fires paled in the distance against the sky, and the stars twinkled more visibly in the still, dewy, unclouded night. Our bonfire was soon but a dull heap of smouldering embers, into which the rollicking urchins vainly poked long sticks, hoping to rekindle a flame; but only a few sparks darted up spasmodically and expired.

Some days later, by previous arrangement, we rode over after dinner to the house of Mr. P——, where we found him waiting, his donkey saddled and bridled. After exchanging a few compliments with his mother and his fair daughter Kleanthé, we dashed off on the road to Sclaviá, Takvore bringing up the rear, mounted on a spirited sorrel mule, and gallantly attired in his new holiday suit the better to dazzle the eyes of the peasant maids.

The first part of our ride wound through the Kampo, but we soon reached the foot of the hill on which the convent of St. Minás is situated. Climbing slowly up the long ascent, we passed the monastery on our left, with its quaint rearward of windmills, that would have ravished the doughty soul of Don Quixote, all turning their long arms round and round, with a languid, sing-song motion, in the fresh breeze that played on the heights. It actually induced a soporific effect on the observer to watch the monotonous old wheat-grinders at their work, as if they had been going thus since Noah came out of the ark, while the dusty and no less sluggish millers leaned against the walls of their respective mills, gazing idly into vacancy.

After a charming ride we entered the bounds of Sclaviá, a straggling district presenting a rugged scenery not found in the Kampo. Grand, hewn-stone villas were still to be seen, but at greater intervals, and the peasantry we met appeared to be of a more primitive order, while their dialect was more corrupted by provincialisms than the Greek in use nearer Port Kastro. As we passed by the fields where the laborers were reaping, they saluted us in true patriarchal style, repeatedly inviting us to dismount and partake of their cheer. We saw one deserted pyrgo whose entrance was commanded by an imposing gate-way from which a long, stately avenue of ancient cypresses led up to the mansion, appearing in their sombre livery like mourners sorrowing in silent majesty for the departed souls who had formerly dwelt there. In another spot we observed a neat little Roman Catholic church nestling among the trees, at the bottom of a shady valley, its campanile lifting a white cross above the embowering foliage.

We finally alighted in the court-yard of a

deserted villa, whose lower story was partially occupied by a decrepit couple, relics of the family which had inhabited it previous to the revolution. We seated ourselves beside a beautiful, mossy tank of clear water, and after supplying our glasses from a spring of remarkable coolness which bubbled up through an aperture in the pavement of the court, Takvore produced some pastries from his saddle-bags, and the old gardener brought us some delicious plums from his little orchard. These were of several species, one of which, of nearly a finger's length, oval shaped, and of a transparent green color, is said to flourish only on the soil of Sclaviá; it is dried for exportation, and is used in the Levant for medicinal purposes.

Words are inadequate to convey an idea of the glorious prospect spread before us. On the one hand the purple outlines of Samos and Ikaria skirted the horizon on the verge of the blue Egean, and still nearer loomed the viny headlands and slopes of Ionia. Scio, lovely as the garden of the Lord, lay at our feet, presenting to the enchanted beholder beautiful varieties of hill and valley, the lights and shadows slowly creeping over the landscape as the sun approached the west. Noble buildings, imposing even in ruins, and antiquated hamlets perched on the hill-tops, diversified the scenery; while, like a setting to the picture, the rugged mountain crags of Scio were bathed in a rosy light. Nor should I forget to mention a dismantled fortification directly in the foreground, — probably a relic of the Genoese, — whose mouldering buttresses were concealed by a profusion of ivy, that made it appear almost a part of the rock on which it was founded.

As we sat there revelling in the prospect, the venerable gardener related to us the tragedy of his house. All the family had collected there on learning that hostilities had commenced at Port Kastro. Not aware of the extent to which the atrocities were carried, they hoped that they might in that remote corner escape the storm. But one morning they heard the cracking of pistols among the neighboring hills, and before they could fly they saw the turbaned cut-throats trooping into the court-yard of the pyrgo. The doors of the house barring ingress to the miscreants, they prepared to deal with their victims by treachery, and summoned the men within to descend and treat for terms of ransom. The latter, if alone, might have defended the building for hours and then died like heroes, but there were their wives and children weeping around them, and they knew that sooner or later the foe must prevail, and then, the fiercer the fight, the more terrible would be the doom that awaited their families. Therefore they chose what appeared the least of two inevitable evils, and went forth to treat. The result is easily foreseen. But one of the adult males escaped to tell the tale, and he was our narrator, the old man before us; the women and children were sold into slavery. One of the boys was afterwards ransomed, and educated in America, and has for many years been practicing medicine in Constantinople.

As we gazed on the wrinkled countenance of the old man and then turned our eyes on the blooming picture below us, a mourning veil seemed to overshadow the island, and the lamentations of those who have fallen by the sword rang in our ears like the notes of a funeral knell.

From Sclaviá we passed through a singular little village reminding one of Bayle St. John's description of the town on the oasis of Sivah. The houses, or rather huts, were low but massively constructed of stone, with very conical, slated roofs, and were frequently connected and strengthened by arches thrown from house to house across the street, giving a subterranean air to the place. Some of these hovels were of considerable age, several bearing date above the doors as far back as the fourteenth century. The villages of the southern part of the island are generally built in this style to protect them from earthquakes.

After quitting this hamlet we entered the mastic villages or cantons, twenty-four in number. The gum produced here has from remote antiquity been one of the staple products of Scio. The mastic or lentisk is a shrub rather than a tree, rarely attaining lofty growth; the gum, a resinous substance, is obtained at the warmest seasons, and is used in large quantities in the harêms of the East for perfuming the breath, as well as to impart an agreeable flavor to water, preserves, or spirits. Since the possession of the island by the Turks, the revenue arising from the mastic of Scio has been hereditarily apportioned to the Sultana Validé, or Queen Dowager, for pin-money.

Soon we passed through a village situated near the sea-shore, in the midst of which arose a rude, ponderous citadel, like a feudal castle, towering far above the huts clustering around its base. This fortalice was erected in the remote past as a place of refuge from the descents of the corsairs who, until a recent period, have infested the shores of the Archipelago. It was on a circumstance connected with these piratical incursions that Mrs. Hemans composed her beautiful poem, "The Bride of the Greek Isle."

As our mules ambled slowly across the public place of the village, we were amused by the various groups of women and children enjoying the approach of evening, spinning before their doors, or chatting around the village fountain as they filled their water-jugs, or playing in the by-lanes. One little urchin two or three years old was sprawling in the road directly in our path, totally unconscious of the approach of our cavalcade; but his mother, rushing from the house with a shriek, seized him by the arm and dragged him aside, at the imminent risk of dislocating that unoffending member.

"Is that your little boy, my good woman?" inquired Mr. P——.

"Yes, thank God! and he's the dearest little creature that ever lived!"

"Aye, that he is indeed; what eyes, what cheeks! may he live!"

"Thanks to you; but spit on his face, Sir; the evil eye, you know, Sir."

Mr. P—— complied with her request, a frequent petition in the East, an emission of saliva being popularly considered a preventive against any injurious admiration or hellish spells.

From this village we commenced our return by another route, which led us to the nunnery of St. Katerina, where our friend, who was acquainted with the prioress, proposed that we should alight. We were ushered into the reception room of the establishment, and were courteously received by the prioress. A demure but comely nun served us to rose preserve and water flavored with mastic. She informed us that she had formerly been named Katinko, but that on taking the veil she had assumed the name of Theosevó, which is, by interpretation, God-fearing. The prioress informed us that at the time there were one hundred and twenty nuns and fifty children under her charge. As it was now growing dark, we declined visiting the school-room and refectory, and took our leave.

After winding sometime over the hills we finally arrived at the mansion of our Greek friend, whence we turned off to our own pyrgo, which we reached about ten, somewhat fatigued but not too much so to enjoy heartily a cup of tea, and thereafter a refreshing slumber.

The day came at last when we must leave our quiet retreat in Scio. Many were our regrets as we packed up our things and sent them on board the vessel that was to bear us away. At midnight, when the long watch-cry of the sentinel on the ramparts of Port Kastro was floating over the calm waters of the strait, we embarked on the steamer *Imperatrice*, that stopped off the port a few moments to take passengers on board.

IX.

HELLAS.

THE Isles of Greece skirted the horizon at sunrise. Scio lay far astern, and Delos, Mycono, Tenos, and Syra were near us on the beam or over the bow. A fresh breeze from the southward furrowed the sea with billows that sparkled in the sun and gave a pleasant motion to the vessel as we paced the quarter-deck and gazed with enthusiasm on the exhilarating prospect. The islands of the Archipelago are generally sterile as seen from a distance, Mytilene, Scio, and a few others excepted, although on nearer approach vineyards may be perceived on the slopes, and the white villages clinging to the cliffs impart that indescribably picturesque effect that is peculiar to scenery on the northern coasts of the Mediterranean ; and whether they are observed close at hand or in the offing, there is always a luminous purple haze suffusing the island peaks, that causes them to seem like enchanted isles floating on an enchanted sea.

We saw very distinctly the convent and hospital of Tenos erected on the spot where a picture of the Virgin was miraculously discovered by means of a holy dream. An annual fair is held there to which Greeks resort from all quarters of the Levant with votive offerings, not a small share of which has been donated by robbers, from the rewards of their profession, for the peace of their souls. With a portion of the large income derived from these sources the poor and the sick are maintained at the hospital. Many astonishing cures are said to have been performed by the sacred ikón, but I am inclined to be sceptical enough to attribute these results partly to the salubrious air of the island.

At noon we anchored in the excellent harbor of Syra, and the difference between Turkey and Greece was at once perceptible. Here we found a homogeneous people and a nation that is renewing its youth, exhibiting, in spite of its backwardness, unmistakable signs of vitality. National individuality here strongly asserted itself, and the increased activity we beheld, gave a kind of stimulus to the mind slightly enervated by the slumberous habits of the dreamy Osmanlee. Syra is a lively city rising on a very steep acclivity, forming a cone of white stone houses terminating at the top by a church.

At dinner our company was reinforced by two silent Englishmen from India, tall, reserved, and bronzed by the sun of the torrid zone, and a Greek gentleman with his wife and two daughters, who were sufficiently attractive to promise an agreeable chat in the evening; for in the Levant and on shipboard a speaking acquaintance is soon formed among entire strangers. But this little plan was nipped by an untimely circumstance. Supposing us ignorant of the Greek language, the ladies at the table discussed the Englishmen with a degree of freedom that would have been embarrassing to those haughty aristocrats if they had been aware of the tenor of the conversation. As I understood all that was said, I was considerably diverted, and at the same time, lest the ladies should be embarrassed by perceiving that their remarks were understood, I was obliged to exercise severe control over the facial muscles; but these were soon put to a stronger test, for the conversation suddenly took an unexpected turn by making the writer the subject of remark. For several minutes I had the opportunity of appreciating the feelings of the man who sees his own obituary in the papers; and after this I was forced to deny myself the pleasure of chatting with the fair gossips in the evening when the full moon was shining on the port, while the band of a Prussian corvette within a cable's length filled the air with delicious strains.

Towards midnight we got under weigh, and sighted the shores of Attica at dawn. It was with strange, tumultuous emotions that I once more beheld my native land. By Salamis, into the Piræus we glided over a sea of glass, until the Acropolis burst on our view flooded with the glory of morning. Impatiently I went ashore, rode over the plain hallowed by so many battles fought for liberty, and found myself again in Athens.

On the morning of my return, with my excellent friend Mr. Constantine, I walked through the Agorá or market-place. I had but to close my eyes and on opening them to fancy myself with a slight effort of the imagination in the Athens so graphically described in the visit of St. Paul: 'All the Athenians and strangers which were there spent their time in nothing else, but either to tell, or to hear some new thing." Eighteen hundred years have passed away since that vivid portraiture of a people was written; the picture remains as a means of comparing the ancient with the modern Athenian, and we find that no essential change has taken place during all these eventful ages, unless it be, possibly, that the vital spark, the admirable genius of ancient Greece, which expired during the Dark Ages, has not yet been rekindled. As I strolled through the market, directly before me arose the Acropolis; nearer, at the head of the street, was the Horologium of Andronicus, vulgarly called the Temple of the Winds; and around me were the Athenians, buying and selling, chatting in busy knots at the corners, and "spending their time in nothing else but either to tell, or to hear some new thing."

In observing these groups, whose profiles and figures recall those who once exercised in the gymnasiums of Athens, I was gratified to see how strong patriotic pride still preserved many of them from exchanging the superb national costume of modern Greece for the stiff and artificial fashions of Paris. With all respect for the flowing robes or the warrior's armor of the Periclean age, it appears to me that the Albanian costume adopted by the Greeks before the revolution and still used by many of them, is the finest dress ever worn by any people. The Highland costume, which somewhat resembles it, is by no means so graceful as this, which consists of a kilt called the fustanella, closely gathered around the waist and hanging loosely to a short distance above the knee in massy folds of snow-white cloth; a long girdle woven of many brilliant tints is wound tightly around the already slender waist; I have seen Athenian exquisites fasten one end of this girdle to a post and then wind themselves up; a crimson or blue vest of woollen stuff embroidered with gold but half conceals the ruffles of the flowing-sleeved shirt, and over this is a jacket similarly adorned; leggins of the same material and color with gold thread buttons and fringe, and a crimson fez long enough to droop by the weight of the heavy blue silk tassel that rests on the shoulder, complete this magnificent costume, unless we add the broad red leathern belt for pistols and daggers buckled over the girdle by the mountaineers or worn in time of war. Such a suit naturally costs too much to be often renewed, and this will probably be the reason why it will eventually go out of date. Say what we will, utilitarianism has the day; but I would not be understood as grumbling against the inevitable laws controlling human tastes as well as actions, and teaching us the advantages of resigning the lesser for the greater good. And yet it is a relief to turn from this age of bronze to that age of gold, when the pursuit of the beautiful for itself alone was not deemed a sign of mental feebleness, when they reared magnificent monuments and composed poetic strains under the inspiration of that love of beauty which is inborn in every genuine and healthful nature. We are now wiser and certainly sadder than they were; we have eaten of the tree of knowledge, and have made the discovery that beauty unwedded with utility is vanity. A poem composed merely from an overflow of poetic feeling without a utilitarian object in view, a romance that does not under a thin disguise undertake to create a moral reform, a picture that does not convey an allegorical lesson, a sumptuous building that is not intended for a state-house or an asylum, is in decidedly bad taste; this is the tendency of the highest writers and thinkers of the day, although of course inferior and untutored minds are yet independent of this creed. There is no doubt that truth, as in a well, lies at the bottom of our modern theory of the beautiful, but I am old-fashioned enough to feel the force of that ancient worship of the beautiful for itself alone, to which men consecrated such immortal creations.

What a relief it is to escape awhile from the whirl and din of this age of steam, and to wander alone by the Theseium, by the Areopagos, through the Propylæa, where every object reminds us of that passion for beauty which animated the soul of the ancient Athenian, and over that pavement which still bears the ruts deeply worn in the marble by chariots before the Christian era; until, on the summit of the Acropolis, the spirit may forget the present, and lose itself in that memorable past which is a living reality to the worshiper of all that is heroic and beautiful in the lives of nations, or in the memorials which they left behind them to create a bond of sympathy between the men of different periods, and to arouse their descendants to the attainment of still loftier heights of glory.

The Acropolis at Athens! how many have described it and how many have visited or read of its astonishing ruins; how many museums and cabinets have been enriched with precious fragments from its inexhaustible treasury of art; how many folios have illustrated its wonders; how many have consecrated their lives to the study of its monuments, or sought to imitate the unapproachable beauty of its sculptures and colonnades; what genius was devoted to its adornment; what genius has been expended in the restoration and preservation of its antiquities; what poetic eloquence has wreathed its venerable battlements with the immortal flowers of poesy! The central spot of ancient civilization, and the point of departure for the legislation, the art, and the literature of subsequent ages, the thoughtful mind "musing there an hour alone" will gain a more earnest appreciation of what man has achieved in the past, and a more steadfast faith in the final success of the Hellenic race and the regeneration of the East.

Standing on the steps of the Parthenon one sees before him the Gulf of Egina, Salamis in the distance, and the harbors of Piræus, Phalarum, and Munychia, to which extended the famous Long Walls. Far off in the dim blue is the Acrocorinthus, Mt. Parnes and the Pass of Philæ are nearer, then Mt. Pentelicus; on the left rises Mt. Hymettus, and inclosed between the mountains and the sea lies the plain of Athens, delicately green with its famous olive groves, or variegated with grain and wild flowers billowing in the breeze, the rich tints of the landscape softened and harmonized by the faint violet haze that pervades the whole. As the low wind sighs through the noble porticoes of the majestic ruins, it brings to the dreamer's mind the scenes of other days, as if it were the murmur of the voices of fallen generations. The long, solemn procession wending its way to the Eleusinian mysteries; or the Panathenaic train marching up from the city below, priests, youths, maidens, heroes, and sages, with chariots and votive offerings, and bearing aloft the sacred Peplus, passing through the magnificent portals of the Propylæa, and sweeping by the Parthenon into the Erectheum; the battles for freedom, the audiences assembled around the Pnyx and swayed by the matchless tongue of Demosthenes,—all this and far more appears vividly to the mental vision.

The antiquities of Athens have been so often described by able scholars that to attempt a new account of them would almost seem like presumption. But I would call the attention of the reader to one very interesting ruin that has been brought to light within comparatively a recent period; this is the celebrated theatre of Bacchus, which has for many centuries been hidden from sight by the layers of earth that have accumulated during past ages and buried it from sight. It is situated at the foot of the Acropolis, on the southern side, adjoining the Odeum of Herodes

Atticus, and is in excellent preservation. The plan is in the form of a semicircle, the galleries rising one above the other and facing the south. The tiers of marble seats are almost as perfect as if quarried yesterday. The first and best circle consists of arm-chairs of Pentelic marble, bearing inscriptions still unimpaired, designating the persons to whom they were awarded. The mayor's seat is in the centre, slightly raised above the others, and with a pedestal at its side which supported a statue. It is noticeable that the priests of ancient Athens were assigned honorable and prominent seats in the first circle. Many splendid fragments have been unearthed, torsos and limbs of statuary that adorned the theatre; a colossal head of Bacchus, the *genius loci*, is conspicuous for its beauty. In this theatre the immortal tragedies of Æschylus, Sophocles, and Euripides, the comedies of Aristophanes, and most of the great plays of Greece were acted before the Athenian multitudes assembled beneath the blue sky of Attica, an awning being extended over them only when the sun was too oppressively warm; little had they to fear of rain in that radiant clime.

There is still another link between ancient and modern Athens which we do not remember to have seen noticed with the attention it deserves. Athena or Minerva, the goddess of wisdom, was the tutelary deity of Athens, and the owl was consecrated to her, doubtless on account of its superior intelligence; such was the resemblance it bore to Minerva that one of her distinctive titles was — owl-eyed. Aware, probably, of their peculiar relation to the goddess, an extensive colony of these mysterious birds settled in Athens at an early period, particularly in the crannies which exist in the rocky sides of the Acropolis, expressly provided, there is reason to believe, by Minerva herself in the immediate vicinity of her shrine, for the accommodation of her feathered votaries. So numerous was this colony that "owls to Athens" became a proverb equivalent to "coals to Newcastle." Great was the respect accorded to the owl by the Athenians; his sapient eyes blink at us from many a well-worn coin and sculpture, venerably ludicrous. But, not satisfied with having his name associated with the goddess of wisdom and his effigy engraved on the masterpieces of Phidias, this cabalistic fowl has ceased not to propagate his species in spite of the strange mutations of time, and the lineal descendants of the owls of ancient Athens continue to remind us that wisdom died not with the ancients. The broad sun of noonday does not seem to disturb their equanimity. Perched on the ruins whose erection their ancestors superintended with lively interest, they wink at the irreverent traveller who visits the Acropolis with an imperturbable gravity that would stare any sensitive nature out of countenance, or flit among the solitary columns of the Parthenon like shades of the departed. One who carefully studies the character and customs of these miniature philosophers, — for they belong to a very minute order of the genus strix, — is half disposed to turn Pythagorean and believe that the souls of the founders of Athens have transmigrated into those plump little fowls, and watch here for the revival of Athenian glory. How long will they have to wait for that day? when shall patience have its perfect work?

Patience must indeed be the motto of the Philhellenist who longs for the restoration of Athens and of Greece; his faith in the progress of the Greeks, and in their energy and disposition to overcome obstacles and rise above their present condition, must often be taxed to the uttermost. Athens has in the last thirty years developed into a charming place of residence, well laid out, the streets broad and cheerful, and the dwellings commodious and suited to the climate. The late queen somewhat atoned for the errors of the Bavarian rule by embellishing her capital; the beautiful gardens she planted form a delightful promenade where all Athens turns out for a stroll towards evening; but the chief improvement she introduced is a fine walk or drive encircling the city and accessible in a few minutes from any quarter of Athens. An easy walk of an hour and a half or less makes the traveller acquainted with the position of the various spots of interest, after which he can proceed to inspect the different localities successively and at his leisure. The society of Athens, both native and foreign, is agreeable and intelligent, including many who have achieved celebrity in war and in letters. But Athens cannot be taken as a specimen of the rest of Greece, which has not made that advance on its condition immediately subsequent to the revolution which there was reason to expect. During my residence in Greece years ago, I went to Mané, in the southern part of the Peloponnesus, the ancient Sparta or Laconia. A small coaster of twenty tons which we hired for the trip took us around Cape St. Angelo. The captain was a Hydriote, and as we were not pressed for time, he of course stopped on the voyage at the island of Hydra to visit his wife: there is no mistaking the Greek sailors of to-day as the descendants of the roving companions of Ulysses. We all went ashore and climbed up the precipitous streets of the town to the skipper's abode, where we were treated to the usual coffee and preserves, and were taken by our hostess into a neighboring chapel to hear vespers before reëmbarking, we being the sole attendants. A terrific thunder-blast took us off the Cape, the sailors fell on their knees and vowed a fabulous amount of tallow candles to St. Nicholas and the Virgin, and we all expected to go to the fishes. My father was going around the same cape some months later in a Greek corvette, when the vessel was struck by a squall; the whole crew of two hundred men came down on their knees, after which they proceeded to take in what sails were left on the yards!

The next day our mariners touched at Elaphonîsé to recruit their exhausted frames with fruit and wine; "to keep their spirits up they poured the spirits down," offering propitiatory libations to Neptune, who at last became pacified, and we finally reached Marathonîsé on the mainland, and rode thence on horseback to a town in Areopolis, where in the family of the Rev. Mr. Leyburn we spent three months. A rough and barren land is Mané, looking as if stones had rained upon it from heaven; and the little wheat raised there is very dark. The bread is almost black, composed of lupins, wheat, and other ingredients, baked hard and only a few times a year. The prickly-pear grows there in great perfection. Many of the people live in castellated towers, visible far out at sea. The houses were formerly built in this style owing to the many feuds amongst the inhabitants. A man has been known to stay in one of these towers ten years, not daring to pass the gate except on a woman's back, for his enemies were ever on the alert, and through the loopholes of their own *pyrgoes* kept their muskets pointed at his dwelling. We returned to Athens by land, through narrow passes and over steep mountain paths infested by brigands, so that at times we were accompanied by a guard of soldiers. The muleteers, until we got out of Mané, were peasant women, who followed on foot. When the mules were going up a steep ascent the women helped themselves along by grasping the tails of the animals, and where they were descending a slippery path they kept the mules from sliding by repeating this action. On a Saturday afternoon in the mountains of Arcadia we were overtaken by a tremendous thunder-storm. At the outset the dry bed of a torrent called Sarandapótamos lay in our path; we had occasion to cross it twenty times that day, and the last time the water had risen to the mule-girths, and threatened to sweep us away. Soaked to the skin, we spent Sunday at the village of Ahoory, in a hut consisting of a stable with a single room over it, which we occupied, and a fire-place without other outlet for the smoke than the door and crevices in the roof.

Such was travelling in Greece then, and such it continues, with but slight changes, to this day. One may now visit Mané in a steamer that runs once a week from Athens; but if he wishes to traverse the country by land he must carry his own bedding and cooking utensils. Hospitality will often be gladly extended to him, but the natives of Greece in their best estate require less to live upon than the European or American, and the masses are content with very primitive fare and lodging. An infinite number of plans for the internal improvement of Greece have been discussed in their legislative assembly, which have afforded ample scope for the display of Hellenic bunkum, but no important results yet appear to the nicest perception, —

> " For he must needs have optics keen
> Who sees what is not to be seen."

Last year three English noblemen landed in Akarnania for a short trip among the mountains; their little excursion cost them three thousand pounds; they fell into the hands of robbers and paid that sum for their liberty. When I was in Greece some months later it was considered safe to ascend Mt. Lykabetus, behind the royal palace, from whence one of the most remarkable views in the Levant may be obtained; it was also considered reasonably safe to venture to Eleusis; but unless the traveller was burdened with a plethora of money and was willing to encourage Greek enterprise by leaving a round sum in some mountain den, he was advised to keep within the immediate neighborhood of Athens. Not that there was then any great probability of being waylaid, for it should be borne in mind that the country was at that time considered comparatively quiet; but these Greeks have very "taking ways," and the tourist in Greece will rarely find a reasonable share of prudence unreasonable. Those who have read Edmund About's "King of the Mountains," but have doubted the truthfulness of its portraitures, may rest assured that as a picture of what it undertakes to represent its faithfulness cannot be surpassed; it is so perfect that it almost amounts to a caricature. Hadgee Stavrós, his hero, represents the Greek bandit as he is, and Byron's Lambró, the corsair described in Don Juan, exhibits the kleft or freebooter of the ante-revolutionary period. Although pursuing the same business, there is a material difference between the two characters not to the credit of contemporary Greeks.

The brigand of Greece is a personage whom time has left to this generation, to remind us, amid the strange mutations of our day, of Robin Hood and his merry men. "Le Roi des Montagnes" is a prose epic, the "Lyttell Geste" of the nineteenth century; the kleft is an historic personage, worthy of mention in the chronicles of the time, a link between our own and former ages. To trace his origin we must look back twelve hundred years to the rise of Mahomet the camel-driver of the desert. Ever since the subjugation of Greece by the Moslems the country has been in a turbulent condition. It was hatred of the Turkish yoke that lent almost superhuman energy to the arm of Iskender Bey; the same impulse inspired the warriors of Sûli to wage perpetual warfare with the Turk; and this spirit it was — a singular blending of religion, patriotism, and lawless freedom — that caused the mountains of Greece to swarm with klefts or banditti at the period immediately preceding the war of independence. There was considerable genuine romance connected with the lives of these mountaineers, who gave rise to some of the little poetry of modern Greece that is worthy of record; their wild, simple, plaintive ballads of love and war seem to retain a spark of Homeric fire.

Many of the prominent leaders in the revolution had been chieftains of note, combining in their lives and character the daring freedom and portly bearing of the feudal lord and the unscrupulous ferocity of the Italian cut-throat. When that heroic struggle was over, and it became unlawful to rob and murder Turks, they found their occupation gone. Some of them settled down into scheming, restless politicians, while others, uneasy, like the sailor who retires from life at sea, sighed for new adventures, sometimes attempting, like Griziôtes, to raise an insurrection, sometimes returning to their evil ways, and, for lack of Turks, occasionally worrying a poor Christian, — with the precaution of keeping their souls safe by a strict attention to the fast-days of Holy Church, and endowing it with costly donations. Facts show that this has proved a profitable and not dishonorable pursuit, as public opinion goes in Greece. But outlaws in Greece once possessed higher motives than those of mere gain, and represented a contest between races and religions, somewhat as Robin Hood and his foresters are supposed to have been representatives of a struggle long maintained between the Saxons and their Norman subjugators. In the Turkish Empire brigandage is a result of weakness, a sign of dissolution, while in Greece it is a relic of past ages destined, we hope, before long to disappear.

Greece is like a man long subject to evil passions and desperate fortunes, who determines on a new course of life, but finds the ghosts of his former hardships and sins continually haunting him and sometimes paralyzing his efforts after reform. She has not yet recovered from her licentious life under the Roman rule, from the monkery of the Dark Ages under the Lower Empire, and from her slavery and predatory warfare under the Turks. Would you ask miracles of her?

"A thousand years scarce serve to form a state;
An hour may lay it in the dust; and when
Can man its shattered splendor renovate,
Recall its virtues back, and vanquish Time and Fate?"

One becomes weary sometimes of hearing the Greeks constantly vilified, and is disposed to inquire whether there is not another side to the question; whether something cannot be adduced in their favor. It is true that their progress since the revolution has been slow, and that they continue to display the vices which have earned for them so ill a reputation; but it should be remembered as suggested above, that some of these evil traits have been fostered if not begotten by long ages of tyranny; in the words of the sage of Concord, —

"He who has no hands
Perforce must use his tongue;
Foxes are so cunning
Because they are not strong."

And there are different grades of vice and virtue even among the Greeks; at Constantinople and Smyrna they are less manly and more corrupt than in the interior of Asia Minor or among the mountains of Macedonia and Lakonia. The accusation of cowardice so often brought up against the modern Greeks, even by such acute and candid writers as

M. About, I do not consider worthy of consideration. It is sufficient to point to the long warfare of the revolutionary period, to its many heroic men and deeds, and to the persistence of the Cretans in their present struggle. Unquestionably poltroons are to be found, and too often modern Greek valor is largely tempered with discretion, but it is the fault of their education rather than their nature; the Greek of our day is no more a coward than any other people of Southern Europe or the Levant. In a regular stand-up fight with well-disciplined troops they may waver, for the bravest irregular soldiery are at a disadvantage in fighting armies thoroughly drilled, but they are at home in their mountain warfare; so is it with the Spanish guerrillas, and they are not considered foes unworthy the steel of brave men. That ancient Greece had its cowards as well as its heroes, is made evident, among other circumstances, by Theophrastus' masterly characterization of cowardice, clearly drawn from life. The Greeks are naturally not a sanguinary race; the intense hatred caused by the cruelties of the Turks has induced them, in fighting with that people, to indulge in terrible excesses by way of retaliation, but they usually have their passions under control sufficiently at least not to make them conflict with their interests. A coup d'état at Athens is not less complete in its results than at Paris, but it is accomplished without bloodshed, — a revolutionary excellence attained as yet by no other people in Christendom.

I well recollect the uprising of 1843. Exasperated by the miserable rule of Otho and the evil counsels of his Bavarian minions, a plot was hatched to wrench a constitution from him, and when everything was ripe the Athenians arose. At midnight the hoofs of horses were heard clanging on the pavement, and the flash of torches gleamed in the streets, as the populace and military hurried towards the palace; and when the amber-colored dawn lighted the Acropolis and the plain of Athens, lo! the king found himself surrounded by his happy subjects, and discovered two field-pieces pointing into the entrance of the royal residence. A constitution was demanded in firm but respectful terms, it being suggested at the same time that, if the request were not granted by four P M., fire would be opened on the palace. In the meanwhile, all Athens was gathered in the open space around the palace, chatting, cracking jokes, taking snuff, and smoking, as if they had assembled to witness a show or hear the reading of a will. Not a shot was fired; no violence was offered or received; and precisely as the limiting hour arrived, the obstinate king succumbed to his besiegers, the charter was granted, and the multitude quietly dispersed to their homes. In less than twenty-four hours the character of the government had changed, and not a drop of blood had been shed; and yet that the importance of the event was not undervalued but was appreciated by all classes, was proved by many circumstances. Two or three days after the crisis, a crowd of boys was seen in the streets, hilarious, and shouting, "Long live the Constitution!" "Well, my boys, what's the matter now?" inquired a bystander. "Oh, our schoolmaster flogged one of the boys, so we rose and flogged the master! Are we not also Greeks? Long live the Constitution!" "Ζήτω τὸ σύνταγμα."

Of the same character was the last revolution in Greece, only still more effective than the former. Otho goes on a royal progress to Napoli; during his absence from Athens there is an uprising of the disaffected, the government is subverted, and his Majesty, finding himself without a throne, does not even revisit his capital, but steps on board ship, returns to the land of his nativity, and betakes himself again to the studies he abandoned to assume the government of Greece. A provisional administration succeeds, during which Prince George of Denmark is elected and crowned! The revolutionists have deposed one monarch and enthroned another, and not a life is lost. Is not this truly a singular people?

Although Greece has failed to make that degree of progress which was expected of her, since her independence, she has still advanced considerably, for which she should have full credit. While very little has been done to improve the means of communication and travel, some attention has been paid to agriculture, for which the Greeks have a native genius; large numbers of olive, fig, and mulberry trees have been planted within a few years, adding materially to the wealth of the little kingdom. The commerce, the tonnage, the population, and the revenues, have also greatly increased. The Greek commercial houses established in all the chief cities of the world attest the commercial ability and thrift of the Greeks. Much attention has also been given to education. Numerous schools, such as they are, have been established, and the thirst for information and the liveliness and versatility which characterize the Greek mind of the present day as two thousand years ago, have stimulated the increase of intelligence among the people; and while no commanding genius has arisen among the modern Greeks to immortalize the period with his writings and elevate the standard of literary taste and thought, the scholars of Athens have done much towards popularizing the classic writers and purifying their noble language from the corruptions and vulgarisms which have crept into it during a long period of oppression, and intellectual pedantry and sloth. At Athens a language is now spoken among the educated not far removed from the exquisite diction of the ancients.

But the trait which is now most salient in the national character and best exhibits the vigor that continues to animate the Greek race and promises the most important results in the future, is the longing for national unity which fires every Hellenic heart from Zante to Trebizond. An example of this feeling is the present enthusiasm for Cretan independence which has aroused the kingdom of Greece. There are the best reasons for saying that this does not arise wholly out of a disinterested love for the Cretans, who are not in good repute even in the Levant. It springs from a sort of Panhellenic frenzy or desire to unite in one government all who speak the Greek language or belong to the Eastern Church. This tendency to assemble the different branches of a race into one powerful and coherent mass seems to be a phenomenon peculiar to this period of the world's progress. We have the Panslavic movement, the struggle for a united Italy, the yearnings for a consolidation of the Germanic nations. Old Father Time is welding the races on his mighty anvil into stronger and more fitting weapons for the advancement of mankind to new battle-fields and new victories over the hosts of superstition and sin. The forward movement may be slow but it is sure.

The national feeling in this direction finds vent in many ways, which too often bring ridicule on the Greeks. The memory of their ancestry and the probability that they may in the future attain to a Hellenic unity glorious beyond any thing previously achieved by their race, gives to every Greek the air of a man who comes from the younger and poorer but still haughty branch of a family of rank, and who in default of other heirs, is about to succeed to the ancestral hall and to a position that will at once raise him from poverty to opulence. This sentiment induces the Greeks to conduct themselves in a manner hardly in keeping with their present power and condition; it enters into the character and bearing of courtier and peasant alike. The bare-footed and bare-headed urchins of Athens are christened after the sages and warriors of ancient Greece, and as soon as they attain to years of discretion they commence the national habit of gasconade, talking of what their ancestors have done, and of what they themselves are destined to accomplish. They are constantly planning expeditions across the frontier, and on the slightest pretext make a dash into Turkish territory, discharge their *tuféks*, and return to retail their exploits in the cafés of Athens. It is trifles like these which have done so much to bring discredit upon Greece, who is like a spoiled child under the guardianship of a number of jealous aunts; any irregularity in the conduct of the foreign relations of that miniature kingdom is attended with complications that well-nigh throw the five great powers into hysteria.

But notwithstanding such follies, there is no doubt that under the surface there is a profound and permanent aspiration for the reunion of the various members of the Greek family, a feeling which pervades all classes; and when it occasionally finds a tangible form of expression, as in the Cretan rebellion, it presents such a character as to elicit our respect and admiration for the Greek race, in spite of their numerous and very grave defects. This Panhellenic enthusiasm is the most vigorous sign of vitality in the Greeks of our age, and will gradually incite them to the accomplishment of the glorious destiny yet in store for them.

It is almost a truism to add that the period when the success of the Hellenes shall be accomplished depends very largely on their own conduct; peculation in all departments of the government, venality, lying, cheating, and want of self-respect on the part of the people, mismanagement in the internal condition of the country, brigandage, and disregard of the laws, are not adapted to encourage national growth and prosperity. But while these are the immediate and most apparent reasons for the tardy progress of the Greeks since the revolution, and are partly accountable on the score of their previous condition, there is a graver cause underlying these secondary causes, to which by far the larger part of the vices of the modern Greek character are clearly traceable, — the bondage of the Greek Church over the conscience of the people. Æsop tells the story of a hawk that entangled its claws in the woolly back of a sheep and then sought to fly up with his prey, but found, instead, that the sheep was too much for him, and he was thus kept down until the shepherds came up and caught him. Not to speak irreverently, the state of Greece is exactly that of the hawk! She is trammeled by the weight of a gross, inert, material hierarchy, and seeks in vain to soar into higher regions.

Let us be just: the Eastern Church, like the Papacy, has had a mission to perform. This has been to furnish a bond of union to the scattered members of a race that long periods of servitude have kept without an independent existence, except as sympathy for the same creed kept alive the yearning for reunion under a government of their own; and it was their faith that finally stimulated the people to rise in 1821 and assert their freedom. During the last four centuries also, the Church afforded the Greeks a religion at least nominally of a more elevated character than the polygamous monotheism of their conquerors. So much credit is fairly due to the Greek Church, but more it has not done. On the other hand, since the revolution it has tended rather to lower than to elevate the moral tone of the Greeks, for the reason that when that event gave a strong stimulus to the national intellect and promised great progress and reform, the conservative authority of the Church over the conscience of the people forbade freedom of thought, and thus checked in its legitimate aspirations, the restless and new-born activity of the nation has sought vent in lower channels. The Church desires Hellenic unity not for the sake of permitting, but rather to prevent, greater liberty of conscience.

There are some among us not devoid of common sense in ordinary matters, who allow their judgment to be warped when they dream of the union of the Eastern and Western Churches. Those who are best informed about the Greek Church, its clergy, its disciples, and its dogmas, not as they might be but as they are, not *in posse* but *in esse*, perceive most clearly the absurdity of the whole scheme. It is a vision fit only for the cobwebbed intellects of those antediluvian dreamers who see no impropriety in putting new wine into old bottles, in throwing the world back fifteen centuries, in binding again the adamantine gyves of superstition over the emancipated soul of the nineteenth century; they are first cousins to Rip Van Winkle.

The writer speaks in no sectarian mood; it is not so much what men believe as what they do which constitutes religion and develops character either good or bad. Transubstantiation and confession may not be correct dogmas, in the estimation of some, but they do not necessarily conflict with the sincere worship of Christ and the observance of the moral law. The creed of the Eastern Church has enough in it calculated to elevate and save its disciples if only put into practice. It is just here that we find the radical difference between the liberal Protestant churches of Europe and America and the corrupt churches of the East; the former regard practice as of capital importance and even more essential than belief in this or that particular formula; the latter consider that blind, unquestioning, and ignorant assent to the truth of prescribed dogmas and rituals takes precedence of practical religion; in other words, they legalize the divorce of faith and works. The consequences are exactly what we see; so long as the Greek acknowledges himself a true son of the Church, and allows, or at least expresses, no doubts that might weaken his allegiance to her, he receives full absolution for all the crimes he chooses to commit; and it is just here that the missionaries take their stand. Their aim is by teaching and example to prove and exhibit the absolute necessity of reducing religion to practice, of infusing moral principle into the character of Greek and Armenian, Jew and Mohammedan;—moral principle, without which no people can permanently prosper, that is the one great thing lacking among all classes and nations of the Levant; once let them realize this appalling fact, and the necessity of supplying this moral void, and a new era will have dawned in the East.

But how are the Greeks to elevate themselves, supposing they become aware of their need of moral improvement; freedom of conscience is the indispensable condition of mental and spiritual growth; and this the laws of Greece, while subject to the dictation and interpretation of the clergy, forbid. The courser of the desert, if caged in an inclosure, will dash fiercely onward until he reaches the extent of his bounds, but then he is forced to curb his impatience and pine in a confinement unworthy his noble spirit; but give him his liberty and he will pursue his rapid career over the prairie, and hail the rising sun with the exultation of the free-born. Thus is it with nations; many have arisen in their might and started on the race; but in mid-career they have been checked by the bonds of religious slavery and have lapsed into nothingness. While the Greek Church controls the execution of the civil laws, and forbids the people to think for themselves, casting those who question its authority into noisome dungeons, Greece cannot and will not make any genuine progress. The people, from their easy disposition and their inquisitive and acquiring tone of mind, are naturally inclined to be liberal-minded; it is the clergy, ignorant, immoral, venal and selfish, who are chiefly responsible for most that is evil in the Greece of our day.

That the missionaries have had any success at all in Greece in spite of so many difficulties, is evidence of the good inclinations of the masses. The books distributed have been read not wholly without affecting public thought and opinion; and the long-continued residence of Dr. King at Athens in the face of much annoyance and persecution, has tended rather to strengthen than to weaken the progress of liberty of conscience and religious freedom. The two excellent Greek missionaries, Messrs. Constantine and Kalopothakes, educated in America and now stationed at Athens, are doing much in a quiet way to disseminate the truth, and influence the public mind, although liable to the penalties of the law if found openly proselyting; they in their turn will have converts to take their place; and the American missions to Greece, practically abandoned as unfruitful, are thus found to have resulted in the establishment of at least two able native reformers in the land. In Mané, where no American missionary has been stationed for many years, the people still remember the missionaries with respect and affection, and have at various times recently welcomed Dr. Kalopothakes with an earnestness and sincerity which could not be entirely repressed by the interference of the civil and clerical authorities.

The Greeks have inherited the beauty, and, to some extent, the heroism and genius of their immortal ancestors; they are acute, genial, and courtly in their manners; the humblest peasant-girl of Attica, holding her rude distaff under her arm and spinning by the road-side as in classic times, has a profile as perfect, a form as graceful, and an address as courteous and yet as unaffected as if she were some princess in disguise — another Perdita scarcely concealed by the picturesque costume of a shepherdess. Their country, essentially poetic on account of the peerless splendor of its mountain crags robed with purple in the superb sunsets of the Egean, the magnificent ruins which crown its hoary steeps, the loveliness of its clustering isles, and the historic associations that hallow every sod and throw an aureole of glory over the land, will be an object to arouse the better emotions of the soul to the end of time.

But it must be confessed that there is little hope of the rapid progress of the Greek race toward a nobler destiny unless the Greek Church undergoes a radical change. The Church must either keep pace with the onward march of mankind, or the Greeks must emancipate themselves from their religious bondage and dare to think and act for themselves; and in either case the condition of their social advancement must be a total separation of Church and State. Without necessarily abandoning the Scriptures and the patristic dogmas, there must be an entire liberation from the corrupt system which has prostituted those Scriptures and those dogmas to its own ends; let each man be allowed to settle with his God the question of his beliefs; let there be no more clerical dungeons, no more censorship of the press; and the sons of Greece will gradually become possessors of those inestimable virtues that underlie the foundations of national prosperity, — truth, honesty, moral courage, order, and freedom; the Muses of Parnassus will awake again from their trance of ages, art and science will thrive as never before, the nation will not rely for its integrity on foreign bayonets, and Greece will again become a power in the world. This may be rather a rose-colored vision; but when we consider what tremendous moral and political revolutions have recently occurred in Italy, Germany, and the United States, such as ten years ago the wildest enthusiast would not have predicted, we feel less sceptical than might otherwise be the case when we contemplate the future of the great Panhellenic movement.

X.

CRETE.

THE Island of Crete requires no aid from contemporary events to arouse the interest of the intelligent reader. There is much in her past history to attract and entertain. "Beautiful for situation," with a glorious climate and noble scenery abounding in stirring landscapes, her mountains became the scene of legend and romance from the earliest period. Jove in his infancy was cradled on the snowy summits of her Idæan crags; Homer sang of her hundred cities, and her hundred prores plowing their way to the Sigean shores, and her hero, Idomeneus, battling "far on the ringing plains of windy Troy." In remote antiquity the Cretans formed a confederacy of miniature democracies, living in tolerable concord, and governed by a code said to have been introduced by Minos, and copied in many of its features by Lycurgus at a later period. But like the Swiss, the Cretans, although sturdy republicans, did not disdain to serve as mercenaries in most of the wars of ancient Greece, while they rarely felt enough Hellenism to side with the other Greeks as allies. Their triremes scoured the seas — the corsairs of old — plundering merchant vessels laden with Tyrian stuffs, the gems of the East, and the grain of the Nile. The legionaries of Rome marched through the gorges of Crete, but failed to reduce the island until after their first army had ignominiously perished.

From the first the islanders developed a love of independence, which has clung to them as a distinguishing and ennobling trait among many vices, and through long ages of oppression. The Byzantines, the Saracens, the Latins, and the Ottomans, have successively held possession of Crete. A band of roving Saracens from Spain touched on the island, and were so captivated by its charms that they returned with forty galleys and plundered the villages; but on seeking the coast to reëmbark, lo! their vessels were in flames. Abu Caab, their leader, had anticipated the famous feat of Cortez; he had covertly set the fleet on fire with a purpose of remaining, and to the clamors of his followers replied: "Of what do you complain? Here is your true country; repose from your toils, and forget the barren place of your nativity." They listened and obeyed, married their female captives, and established a city which they called Candax, a name since corrupted to Candia, and incorrectly applied to the whole island. For one hundred and thirty years their rovers swept the seas, and revived the ill reputation of Crete as a nest of pirates. With the exception of the inhabitants of Kydonia, the Cretans at this period embraced Islamism, the creed of their conquerors.

In 960 Nikephoros Phokas, one of the few military heroes who relieved the decline of the Byzantine throne from its disgraceful inefficiency, laid siege to Candia. Seven months were consumed before the walls of a city destined in a later age to sustain the most protracted siege known in history; and even after the storming of the defenses, a hand-to-hand conflict was maintained in the streets before the place fell into the hands of the Greeks, and with it the whole island. All the Cretans were now baptized into the Greek Church, and Nikephoros was rewarded with a triumph at Constantinople and the purple.

Baldwin, the crusader, was the successor of the Byzantines in Crete; then came the Genoese and the Count of Montferrat, who sold Candia to the Venetians for 10,000 marks.

For three centuries the Queen City of the Sea held undisturbed sway over the valleys of Crete, one of the brightest gems in her diadem. But in an evil hour the Sultana Kesém, the mother of Ibrahím Sultan, who by her genius ruled both her son and the Ottoman Empire, conceived the scheme of subjugating Crete. She was seconded in her project by the Grand Vizier, Yusoof Pashâ. A Dalmatian by birth, he was the natural enemy of Venice. While still a barefoot urchin running about the streets of Vrania, his native place, he attracted the attention of a Turkish official riding through the town, who carried him off to Constantinople. With good looks and ready tact and talent at his command, he mounted the successive steps so often trod by those who rise from the lowest grades of society to eminence in the courts of the East, and in due time became Grand Vizier or Prime Minister, and second in power only to the Sultan himself. When he had reached this perilous height he still cherished his hereditary hatred toward the Venetians, and gave a willing ear to the plans of the Queen Mother. To conquer Crete would be to ravish from Venice one of her principal sources of revenue and prestige, and overthrow one of the bulwarks of Christendom. Appointed Generalissimo of the land and naval forces of the expedition, and married to the Sultan's daughter before his departure, Yusoof landed on the shores of Crete with a hundred thousand men. The island was speedily overrun, and Canéa, the capital, captured after a three months' siege, and Yusoof Pashâ then returned to Constantinople for supplies, and to refit his armament for the reduction of the stronghold of Candia; his enemies chose to make the Sultan believe in his unfaithfulness to his command.

"Return to Crete at once, or die!" were the words with which the capricious monarch welcomed his triumphant general.

"My liege," responded Yusoof, astonished at his master's unreasonable demands, "you are unversed in naval affairs; our galleys have no rowers, and ships cannot put to sea without oars."

"Wretch!" cried Ibrahím, "do you presume to teach me?" Then turning to an attendant, said, "Bring me his head!"

The fate of Yusoof was but the lot of half the Grand Viziers of Turkey, some of them men of commanding intellect and magnanimous character; his career is only one of many instances in her history of men who from low degree have soared to the second place in the realm, poised on that dizzy eminence a month, a year, perhaps a decade, and then fallen in an hour like an eagle gazing on the sun, pierced to the heart by the fatal arrow, and in a moment dropping lifeless to the depths below.

For many years longer the war in Crete and the siege of Candia lingered without reaching a decisive result, until the accession of Mahomet the Fourth. His favorite wife Gulmish, was a Cretan by birth, and desired the island as an appanage whose revenues should swell her allowance of pin-money. Achmét Kuprilee, the second of that name, and the greatest of Turkey's Grand Viziers, having added a large slice of Christian territory to the Ottoman Empire, notwithstanding a defeat at St. Gothard, was desirous of giving the finishing touch to his administration by the conquest of Candia.

Morosini, one of the best soldiers of the time, held the place with the flower of the Christian chivalry; and during the siege the garrison was reinforced by frequent arrivals of heroes from all parts of Christendom, anxious to break a lance in this apparently final grapple with the Antichrist. Vauban, the great engineer, and many others of less note, fought behind the seemingly impregnable battlements of Candia, and repelled the oft-repeated assaults of the Janizaries, the most redoubtable warriors of those bloody times.

On one occasion the Duke de Beaufort arrived from France with many gentlemen and powerful reinforcements. Hardly were they landed when, rash and enthusiastic, and disdaining the advice of the experienced Morosini, they sallied out against the Janizaries. But few ever returned, and the Duke de Beaufort never reappeared : Kuprilee made search for his body, but in vain. As on the defeat of Don Roderic, legends were long floating about the island that, humiliated by his reverse, the lost Duke had escaped to the mountains, and was seen at intervals dwelling in the caves, a hermit devoted to penitence and prayer, until sight and memory of him alike passed away.

In September, 1629, two years and three months after Kuprilee opened the trenches, the city fell, the blockade of the place having been maintained for twenty-three years. Over 30,000 Christians and 120,000 Turks were sacrificed during the siege, and the defense has been a model in the conduct of many a subsequent defense. The conquest of Candia was the last great triumph of the Ottoman arms, and it has remained in the hands of the Turks to this day, a period of two hundred and thirty-eight years.

The Turks divided the island into three pashalics or satrapies, and would seem to have taken stronger root there than in most of their Christian possessions. They have intermarried with the Greeks, and, by reason of religious oppression, many of the Christians have, during the lapse of ages, nominally embraced Islamism; although, as a general thing, these proselytes have practiced their old rites in secret, and transmitted the observance of this double religion to their posterity. The reader will be reminded by this circumstance of those Moors of Spain who became outwardly Catholics after the fall of Granada, but who practiced Mohammedanism in private, instances existing even to our time. So intermixed had races and religions become in some parts of Crete, that it gave rise to a proverb still current in the Archipelago when reference is made to the Cretans: Τοῦρκος ἔισε, Μουσταφά; Τοῦρκος ἔιμαι μά τήν Παναγιὰ, which is by interpretation, "Are you a Turk, Mustapha? I swear by the Holy Virgin I am a Turk." As religion in the Levant has more to do with nationality than race, to be a Turk is to be a

Mussulman, and for a Mussulman to swear by the Virgin Mary is an impossibility anywhere but in Crete, where many of the nominal Turks are secret Christians.

Notwithstanding this mixing of races, the Christians of Crete have been treated with an oppression rare even under the Ottoman rule, and it has served rather to stimulate the vices inherent in the Cretan character — impatience of law, venality, cunning, and treachery; it has taught them also their mode of bush-fighting common to most of the modern Greeks, and so like Indian warfare, — hiding behind a thicket, and thence blazing away at the foe. The narrow gorges of the Cretan mountains afford excellent facilities for this kind of tactics, which is by no means incompatible with genuine valor; but in the case of the modern Greek it has become such an inborn characteristic, that he is liable to lose his presence of mind if he cannot rest his musket on the edge of an earth-work, or the crotch of an old olive-tree.

On the southern side of Crete is a small canton called Sphakia, whose inhabitants differ in some respects from the other Cretans. They are supposed to represent the Pelasgic aborigines, who peopled the island before the

Hellenes appeared on the stage of history. Mostly shepherds, and only a few thousand in number, they have always maintained a semi-independence of the Turkish yoke, like the Maniotes, the descendants of the ancient Spartans, and the sturdy Armenian mountaineers of Zeitoon in Asia Minor — subdued only within a few years, after centuries of stubborn resistance. Often defeated, the Sphakiotes as often escaped to the mountains, to return to their villages on the departure of the invader, and resisted payment of tribute to the time of the Greek revolution.

When that war broke out the Greek cruisers appeared off the island; but after the first panic was over the Turks became so exasperated that they began to massacre the Christians. The Sphakiotes having scoffed at a summons to give up their arms, — being encouraged to such a course by their hero Mellidóri, — the Turks prepared to go against them; but as they waited for the conclusion of the annual festivities of Baïrám, the Sphakiotes collected a force of 1200 muskets, and defeated the Turks at Looló. Another check, received at the hands of the brothers Kormoulee, so enraged the Moslems that they massacred over a thousand of both sexes in the city of Candia and elsewhere, including the ten bishops of Crete.

The Kormoulees were a remarkable family. They belonged to the most influential of those Cretans to whom we have alluded, who had outwardly embraced Islamism but practiced in secret the rites of the Greek Church. Before the breaking out of the revolution they had seriously contemplated abjuring their Mohammedanism, although martyrdom would be the certain result. But the priests whom they consulted advised them to postpone such a step as it might precipitate a massacre of the Christians, and be productive of vast suffering. The revolution offered the Kormoulees the opportunity they desired. They at once threw off the Turkish yoke and religion, and entered with such zeal into the contest, that at its close, of sixty-four males numbered in the family, only two survived.

During the summer many combats took place, in which Antonio Mellidóri was conspicuous on account of his bravery and unwavering courage. Before the breaking out of the revolution he had spent some months travelling through Asia Minor and the Archipelago, preparing the Greeks for the approaching revolt. On the 18th of July the Turks were routed with great loss at Askoopi, near Retymo, leaving their baggage and artillery on the field. But the Sphakiotes, after plundering the plains on the northern side of the Idæan slope, returned to Sphakia to divide the booty, which movement enabled the Turks to storm the entrenchments of Therison; and in the September following, an army of about 10,000 Janizaries, guided by a treacherous priest, entered the Sphakiote canton, burned the villages, and drove the people of that and the neighboring districts into the mountains or on board of their coasters. Lack of provisions, however, soon compelled the invaders to retreat to their fortified towns, where the Christians, who had been hitherto spared, were now put to the sword. During this period of the insurrection an enthusiasm pervaded the Cretans which, had it continued, might have enabled them to hush the clamors of discord, and achieve their freedom. During an attack on Therison the Greek women animated their defenders by their presence, and supplied them with fruits and drink; a peasant-girl, carrying a jar of water on her shoulder, had it broken by a ball; but undaunted, she went on to the Greek lines with a basket of grapes.

At this time Mellidóri and Zervas were despatched to the Morea to procure reinforcements and ammunition, and a military leader to assume general command of the Cretan forces. It was but a small supply of powder that they could obtain, but Michael Comnenus Affendooli was appointed to the Cretan department, and arrived at Loutró in November. In the mean time the insurgents had reappeared and laid siege to Canéa, and after cutting the water-pipes that led into the city, reduced the garrison to great straits. But, with the inconstancy so characteristic of irregular soldiery, and particularly of Greek *palikars*, when the rainy season set in the besiegers fell back.

Affendooli was well received by all classes, and seems to have been a man of fair administrative capacity; but, whatever might have been his military talents, he certainly was but ill qualified to conduct the partisan warfare of the Cretans, and control the rude, unstable spirits under his command. The Sphakiotes — brave but treacherous, and despising the other Cretans, or lowlanders, as they called them — required a leader of consummate skill and iron hand.

During the winter considerable supplies and reinforcements arrived, and the Cretans took the field early in the year with a force of near 7000 men, 2400 under General Papadáki, in the western part of the island; 3000 under

Rousso and other chieftains, near the centre; while Antonio Mellidóri guarded the defiles of Asprovooni with a partisan band varying in number from 200 to 1000, but making its mark wherever it struck, until the fame of Mellidóri rang from one end of Crete to the other — a name to kindle the courage of his fellow-countrymen, and fill the heart of the Turk with terror.

But to oppose the Candiote forces the Ottomans had from 20,000 to 25,000 men well provided with all the munitions of war, besides twenty-seven strongholds, and the neutrality of a good portion of the islanders — for many of the Cretans remained indifferent to the cause for which their brethren were in arms; so that the contest from the outset had a very one-sided appearance, by no means reassuring to the insurgents. However, the blockade of Canéa, for siege it could not be called, was resumed with some prospect of success, and the city would have fallen if there had been more concert in the disposal of the Cretan army. But Affendooli was more skillful in wording proclamations than manœuvering battalions, and the Cretans themselves, by their own misconduct, brought matters for a time to a crisis unfavorable to their independence.

Antonio Mellidóri, by his many exploits and disinterested patriotism — patriotic where genuine patriotism was so rarely a dominant principle, — had won the friendship of the commander-in-chief, and had been promoted. This gave umbrage to the turbulent Sphakiotes, whose little souls regarded the contest as only a question whether the Sphakiote or the Ottoman should be tyrant of Crete. A band of Sphakiotes in the command of Mellidóri sacked the hovel of a defenseless old woman, and the captain compelled the robbers to restore the spoil; but as they did so they exclaimed "that his tomb was open," which means in the figurative language of the East, that his doom was sealed. A plot to assassinate him was concocted by the Sphakiotes; Mellidóri's own brother-in-law, Anagnósti, and Captain Rousso, being the principals in this iniquitous scheme. Antonio having crowned his previous exploits by capturing a Turkish village and exterminating the garrison, was invited to a feast by Rousso and Anagnósti, where he was to receive the congratulations of his countrymen for his victory. As the roasted lamb disappeared, and the wine began to circulate, Rousso sought to pick a quarrel with his guest; but failing in this, attempted to slay him, on which Mellidóri mounted and departed; but his brother-in-law followed and besought him to return, offering to bring about a reconciliation. In the act of embracing him Rousso plunged a dagger into his bosom.

The Turks fired a salute on learning of the fall of their great enemy; Mellidóri's friends quit the camp in great indignation; and Rousso being cashiered, all his adherents also left; and the insurgent army was so much reduced that all operations in the pashalíc of Candia were brought to a stand. Mellidóri was one of the few heroes of the Greek revolution whose fame is untarnished by the imputation of sordid ends: the purity of his aims, the breadth of his views, the noble simplicity of his character, and the valor he displayed during his brief military career, remind us of Aristomenes, Leonidas, and other heroes of ancient Greece. He was worthy of a wider influence and a longer life, crowned by deeds more lasting in their consequences to posterity than any he was allowed to achieve. Miss Mulock, in a volume of romantic sketches written years ago, has a spirited tale founded on the exploits of the Cretan hero, although it is not entirely reliable as a historic narrative.

In April Colonel Balesto arrived in Candia

with a band of Samians, and was ordered to the command of the district of Retymo. Instead of the army promised him, he found at Kogsaré a paltry 800, but succeeded in raising the force to 1200; but on attempting a reconnoissance his men began to fall away, and the approach of Easter rather tended to encourage desertion. (N. B.— When the Greeks begin to think less of their one hundred and fifty holy days, and attach more value to matters of importance, there will be more hope of their progress and success as a nation.) In the mean time the Ottoman forces opposing Balesto were increased, but notwithstanding were worsted in an engagement on the plain of Kastello. As the days went by, and it became more and more apparent that the increasing scarcity of provisions would leave him without a man, Balesto resolved to hazard an attack on the Turkish intrenchments. The Turks were about 4000 strong; and by great effort Balesto contrived to collect about the same number of men for the emergency; for the irregular Cretan soldiery are in the habit of collecting and dispersing rapidly. At the last moment he was informed that his men had only six cartridges apiece. To attack under these circumstances was folly; and messengers were despatched to Sphakia for ammunition. At this juncture the Turks quit their works and fell on the Greeks; for three quarters of an hour the combat was evenly balanced, but was finally decided by the treachery of the Sphakiote contingent, who had taken a prejudice against Balesto, and, as is asserted, had sworn his destruction. In the heat of the fight they fled; and Balesto fell into the hands of the Turks, who cut off his head and his right arm. This narrative will give the reader some notion of the way in which the Cretan rebellion was conducted, and how hopeless was the contest from the outset unless foreign intervention could solve the problem, which it was beyond the capacity of the natives to grapple successfully.

To go into the details of the campaign of 1822 and 1823 would be a thankless task. It is sufficient to say that Affendooli was obliged to resign his command, and Admiral Tombazi, a noted seaman of Hydra, was chosen to succeed him. Alternate victories and defeats, and equal cruelty and bad faith, characterized the fortunes of both sides, until the perpetual quarrels of the Cretans were taken advantage of by Mustaphâ Bey, who gave them a notable defeat at Amoorgelee from which they never recovered. Before going into winter-quarters the Ottomans ravaged the island, and either put to the sword or sold into slavery over 10,000 Cretans. At Mellidóni three hundred souls sought refuge in a cavern; Mustaphâ Bey, after attempting to enter the cave in vain, and unable effectually to close it, ordered heaps of brushwood to be piled before the mouth and set on fire; not one of the poor unfortunates escaped. Some weeks later six Christians, who had relatives and friends among the victims, ventured into the cave to learn their fate: so overcome were they by the horrible spectacle that met their eyes, that one of them never again raised his head, but died nine days after, and another succumbed in twenty days to the shock he had sustained. All but the Sphakiotes laid down their arms; multitudes of the Christians emigrated to other islands, and the insurrection was apparently at an end. In the spring the Ottomans swept the island with 20,000 men; and the Sphakiotes, out of hatred to the "Lowlanders," who would not submit to their leadership, entered into private terms of capitulation. While many burrowed in the caves of the mountains or fled to the neighboring isles, thousands met with slavery or death, and the chains of Crete were forged stronger than ever. It is some consolation to our ideas of justice to know that the Sphakiote captains were rewarded for their treason with a dungeon, among them Rousso, the murderer of Mellidóri.

Off the western coast of Crete is a small islet named Grabûsa, crowned by an impregnable fortress, and this was surprised by a handful of Cretans in 1825, and many of those who had fled from Candia returned and settled on this castellated rock; but so thickly were they collected there that starvation carried them off by thousands, and many of the survivors left. However, the strength of the fortress and the difficulty of blockading it, suggested to two clever Cretans, named Antoniádes and Económos, the feasibility of turning it into a piratical rendezvous. The Cretans, as has been before observed, have always taken kindly to this infamous craft. The aforementioned brace of knaves purchased a schooner which made a very successful voyage; and stimulated by this interesting result, a number of Sphakiotes living there fitted out another vessel, and the example was speedily followed by exiles connected with the first families of Crete. A quasi government was established, assuming to represent the four divisions of Crete, and dignified by loud-sounding titles, — the whole under the direction of Económos and Antoniades, who, however, took good care to keep behind the scenes while they pulled the wires. In order to mask their knavery, a band occasionally landed on the coast of Crete, and returned with a great flourish of trumpets after worrying the life out of a few poor Turks, all of which was carefully reported, whereby Philhellenic benevolence was imposed upon and amerced in considerable sums for the support of the war of independence in Crete! In the mean time affairs went on swimmingly with our picarooning adventurers. Their success attracted shoals of villains from all parts of the Archipelago, every person on the rock becoming a shareholder in a joint-stock company organized to plunder the commerce of all nations, including that of the Greeks themselves. Several hundred dwellings arose within the castle, and the company owned, as part of its stock, a force of forty-eight brigs and schooners. Warehouses were erected for storing the captured goods, and the wine-shops rang with the revelry of the roystering crews. The isle swarmed with brokers purchasing the stolen property, and the buccaneers of the

Spanish Main seemed to have come to life again in the Egean; although it is doubtful whether such a complete system of piracy was ever before organized, for the Greeks are shrewd beyond the shrewdest in business matters, the chief difficulty being that they are often so shrewd as to practice dishonesty when there is no occasion for it, and thereby in the end overreach themselves. It is not our purpose, nor do our limits allow us, to dwell longer on this disgraceful episode in the Greek revolution. Impelled by the threats of the European admirals in those seas, and by other reasons, the freebooters finally gave themselves seriously to the work of reviving the insurrection in Crete. Two thousand mercenaries were procured, and, with about as many from Grabûsa, were landed at St. Nicholas. After various fortunes, this, like similar attempts, failed on account of the feuds existing between the Christians recruited from different portions of Crete. In the interval a squadron of English and French men-of-war, comprising nine sail, and with a detachment of infantry on board, appeared off Grabûsa. The artful negotiations that now occurred, the burning of that part of the piratical fleet which had not absconded in time, the loss of the *Cambria* frigate, and the utter uprooting of this piratical nest, form a curious narrative. That the overthrow of Grabûsa was not an easy task, may be inferred from the fact that there were at least 2500 desperate fighting men behind the fortifications.

After the fall of Grabûsa Hadjee Mihâlly, a cavalry officer of some note in the Greek revolution, who had stopped at Grabûsa on his way to Crete, with a corps of Roumeliotes, landed on the Sphakiote coast, but received assistance neither in the way of provisions nor men. Reduced to great distress, he finally surprised a Turkish detachment, routed them, and captured among other plunder, 20,000 sheep, with which he returned to his stronghold of Franco Castello, an old Venetian fortress on the coast. On this the Turkish general, Mustaphâ Pashâ, marched on Franco Castello with over 5000 men and two pieces of artillery. As the captured sheep filled the courtyard of the castle, Hadjee Mihâlly posted all his force, numbering about 700 men, behind low earth-works called tambooria. Then, to quote from a quaint, forcible Cretan ballad on this battle —

"Offering up another prayer,
The cross's sign he made;
His pistols next he duly took,
And in his girdle laid.

"Scarce had he vaulted in his seat,
When wept his charger good;
And then he understood full well
His death it did forebode.

"He offered up another prayer,
And in his saddle sate:
Then onward spurred his trusty steed
From out the castle gate."

Scarcely were his preparations made, when the Turks charged on his works. One redoubt was held by Captain Kyriakooly with one hundred picked men, who tied their legs together in a chain with their girdles, and swore to hold the spot or die. They all fell at their posts but one, who fled; and long after a row of skeletons could be seen bleaching there, bound with shreds of weather-worn girdles. Hadjee Mihâlly was cut to pieces; two hundred and seventy Roumeliotes escaped into the castle, where they found themselves with meat enough and to spare, but no water. They were forced to surrender, and on giving their parole not again to serve against the Sultan in Crete, were provided with provisions, their wounded were carefully tended, and they were allowed to sail away. The whole affair, so heroic on the part of the vanquished, so generous on the side of the victor, is the most interesting episode of the kind in the Greek revolution.

As if to give the other side of the picture, the Sphakiotes — who would not fight when others were ready, but fought when their valor could be of little use — now turned out, and held the passes by which Mustaphâ Pashâ must return. Without heeding the amnesty he proclaimed, they persisted until they reduced him to great extremity. At this crisis, when the consummation of Cretan independence hung in the balance, Mustaphâ, aware of Sphakiote cupidity, summoned a council of war in which it was decided to abandon all the baggage to the enemy. The bait took. Dazzled by the sight of so much plunder, the Sphakiotes seized the spoil before them but allowed the Ottoman army to escape, and with it freedom fled from their grasp for indefinite ages. They were unworthy of the immortal gift which was offered to them, and it was withdrawn.

Enough has been written in the above narrative to prove that at that period Crete and the Cretans were hardly prepared for independence, although they deserved it equally with other Greeks, and should not have been excluded when the treaty of peace was signed. Whether they are now ready to guard the gift of liberty with "sleepless vigilance," is a question to be decided by their own conduct. They cannot be more miserable than they are under the cruel domination of the Turks, and since it is highly improbable that they can unassisted do more than to protract the struggle, it is proper that the European powers should at least offer their mediation to the Porte, and that the public charity should be extended to the suffering non-combatants. The consolidation of Crete with the Greek nation cannot fail to be beneficial to both; Crete under the Turk is like a prisoner chained to a dead man and struggling for release from the fearful union. Crete under the Greek rule will spring to a new existence and develop new energies; but the degree of progress she will make in that improved condition will depend upon the Greek Church, and the amount of religious freedom allowed, as has been before observed. Cretan Christianity is of a very low order. Some idea of this may be gathered from the fact that during their last war the Turkish women captured were very frequently butchered, as it was considered a lesser crime to thus dispose of them than to have the Christian warriors incur the perilous sin of intercourse with unbaptized females!

It is not for what they are that the Cretans

inspire us with interest in their cause, but for what they are capable of becoming in future ages, when possessed of civil and religious liberty, which can alone give an enduring form to the results of their present exertions. That these exertions will result in the immediate emancipation of Crete from the Turkish yoke is naturally a matter of uncertainty; but they will at least have the effect of weakening the power of the oppressor and of ameliorating the condition of the oppressed, and render the ultimate union of Crete with the Kingdom of Greece a problem destined to be happily solved before many years have elapsed.

THE END.

www.ingramcontent.com/pod-product-compliance
Lightning Source LLC
LaVergne TN
LVHW010233110826
845151LV00004B/1279